Our Victorian Education

Blackwell Manifestos

In this new series major critics make timely interventions to address important concepts and subjects, including topics as diverse as, for example: Culture, Race, Religion, History, Society, Geography, Literature, Literary Theory, Shakespeare, Cinema, and Modernism. Written accessibly and with verve and spirit, these books follow no uniform prescription but set out to engage and challenge the broadest range of readers, from undergraduates to postgraduates, university teachers and general readers – all those, in short, interested in ongoing debates and controversies in the humanities and social sciences.

Already Published

Our Victorian Education

Dinah Birch

Blackwell
Publishing

BLACKWELL PUBLISHING
350 Main Street, Malden, MA 02148-5020, USA
9600 Garsington Road, Oxford OX4 2DQ, UK
550 Swanston Street, Carlton, Victoria 3053, Australia

First published 2008 by Blackwell Publishing Ltd

1   2008

Library of Congress Cataloging-in-Publication Data

Birch, Dinah.
    Our Victorian education / Dinah Birch.
        p. cm.
    Includes bibliographical references and index.
    ISBN 978-1-4051-4505-3 (hardcover : alk. paper)—ISBN 978-1-4051-4506-0 (pbk. : alk. paper)
1. Education—England—History. 2. Education—England—Philosophy. I. Title.
    LA631.7.B57 2008
    370.941′09034—dc22

                                        2007026128

Set in 11.5/13.5pt Bembo
by SPi Publisher Services, Pondicherry, India
Printed and bound in Singapore
by C.O.S Printers Pte Ltd

The publisher's policy is to use permanent paper from mills that operate a sustainable forestry policy, and which has been manufactured from pulp processed using acid-free and elementary chlorine-free practices. Furthermore, the publisher ensures that the text paper and cover board used have met acceptable environmental accreditation standards.

For further information on
Blackwell Publishing, visit our website at
www.blackwellpublishing.com

Contents

Contents

Preface

Entering the twenty-first century has made the Victorians seem further back in history. But we still live in their light, and in their shadow. Because their legacies are everywhere, we hardly notice them. They built the political, economic and social frameworks that support our lives. They opened the way to equality and independence for women. They instituted the democratic system that handed a measure of political power to the labouring poor. They compelled religion to redefine itself in the face of science and free-thinking scholarship. Their advances in medicine, public health, transport and communications transformed day-to-day life for the bulk of the British population. They founded the great cities, the military and political power and the manufacturing bases that have defined our national identity. They shifted our population density and gave us new jobs. By the end of the nineteenth century, for the first time in history, significantly more people had urban rather than rural homes. It was the Victorians who invented our world.

This does not mean that they are the benevolent authors of all modern blessings. Complex, fractious and troubled, they also devised many of our most recalcitrant difficulties. A reluctance to agree among themselves is among their most persistent characteristics. This is certainly true of their ideas about teaching and learning. It is my argument that their enduring influence is especially potent in this area, which was revolutionized by their reforms. But I do not want to claim that this preoccupation amounts to a unified body of thought.

The Victorians were deeply divided in their views on who should be teachers, who should be taught, how the teaching should be done and what was to be learned. Conflicts over religion, gender and class are never far from this story, and my exploration of their pedagogic thinking will repeatedly return to their inability to disentangle the tasks of education from questions about the making of clergymen, or Christians, or ladies and gentlemen.

And yet I want to suggest that we can still profit from looking back to the Victorians, as we struggle with our own educational problems. This is a book about the ideals that shaped Victorian schooling, the divisions within those ideals, and their continuing association with our dilemmas. It explores these issues as they are reflected in a variety of texts. I have not assumed that all of my readers will be familiar with the books I discuss, for I hope that my arguments will interest those who are not specialists in this field. Though my approach is both historical and literary, it has not been my intention to provide a detailed history of Victorian education, nor a comprehensive account of the relation between teaching and literature in the period. My aim is more personal, and more contentious. I believe that an acknowledgement of our Victorian inheritance will be salutary, in part because we are inclined to forget how decisively it has influenced us. We have not yet resolved disputes that are rooted in the history of the nineteenth century. They get in our way, as they got in the way of the Victorians. But I also want to argue that we should remember what drove the Victorians' belief in the value of education. They understood that it was more than a matter of social or economic advantage, or even the transmission of knowledge. It could change lives at the deepest level. John Ruskin puts it simply: 'You do not educate a man by telling him what he knew not, but by making him what he was not.'[1] Every thinking adult has some experience of education, and we know Ruskin was right. And yet it is clear that schooling is increasingly hampered by the very systems that we have created to further its work. It is an expensive and laborious business, and we want careful management to ensure that it is responsibly delivered. But it is always more than a business.

It cannot be wholly measured and controlled by systems, no matter how scrupulously they are calculated to guard against failure.

The Victorians, for all their quarrels, affirmed the creative force of education again and again. We can learn from their conviction. Anarchy does not promote learning, but unremitting regulation will not do it either. It is a human process, involving intellect, imagination, spirit and feeling, and it is inseparable from personal commitment. John Henry Newman's assertion, that 'each of us has the prerogative of completing his inchoate and rudimental nature, and of developing his own perfection out of the living elements with which his mind began to be',[2] remains true for us. Young people will not succeed unless they can take risks, and make mistakes. They must grow as individuals, sometimes in ways that no system can predict or direct. We are always in danger of losing sight of these ungovernable facts, and the Victorians too would often neglect them. But they constantly regained their courage. We need that vitality now. It is the purpose of this book to suggest why we cannot do without it, and how its energy might be restored. In this, as in other challenges at the heart of our culture, the Victorians can still help us. They have been this way before.

Acknowledgements

This book could not have been written without a generous period of research leave granted by the School of English at the University of Liverpool, and I am grateful for my colleagues' support. Elements of my argument have been presented at the Universities of Lund, Newcastle, Oxford, Rutgers and Sheffield, and contributions from those who came to listen have been invaluable. I've also benefited from opportunities to discuss education and literature at the annual conferences of the British Association for Victorian Studies. Many friends have been unstinting with their help, and I would like to thank Phil Davis, Rowena Birch, Sid Birch, Katy Hooper, John Carey, Francis O'Gorman and Chris White for much good advice, practical assistance and cheerful encouragement. Thanks are also owed to Al Bertrand, and to his associates in Blackwell, Rosemary Bird, Emma Bennett and Karen Wilson, who have been the most considerate allies. An earlier version of my thoughts on George Eliot has appeared in the *George Eliot Review*, and gratitude is due to the George Eliot Fellowship for permission to reproduce this material. Lastly, I would like to acknowledge my students, past and present, from whom I have learned so much.

Chapter 1
Defining Knowledge

The Spread of Education

The Victorians invented education as we understand it today. We are accustomed, of course, to believing the opposite. The idea of the austere Victorian schoolroom figures as a contradiction of all that a modern educationalist stands for. Images of deprivation and hypocrisy come to mind – burnt porridge in Jane Eyre's harsh school, or the grotesque parody of education in Charles Dickens's *Nicholas Nickleby*:

Obedient to this summons there ranged themselves in front of the schoolmaster's desk, half-a-dozen scarecrows, out at knees and elbows, one of whom placed a torn and filthy book beneath his learned eye.

'This is the first class in English spelling and philosophy, Nickleby,' said Squeers, beckoning Nicholas to stand beside him. 'We'll get up a Latin one, and hand that over to you. Now, then, where's the first boy?'

'Please, sir, he's cleaning the back-parlour window,' said the temporary head of the philosophical class.

'So he is, to be sure,' rejoined Squeers. 'We go upon the practical mode of teaching, Nickleby; the regular education system. C-l-e-a-n, clean, verb active, to make bright, to scour. W-i-n, win, d-e-r, der, winder, a casement. When the boy knows this out of book, he goes and does it.'[1]

This is unforgettable, but it is also misleading. Victorian education was not simply a matter of victimized children and brutal school-masters. Much more often, it was a vision of hope, promising to transform the misery of impoverished minds into the prospect of a richer life for every child.

It was the Victorians who first conceived of education as a formal process that would be crucial to the life of the nation and all of its citizens, with prescribed courses of study, and outcomes measurable by examination. Our sense of what matters most in teaching and learning is shaped by legacies of nineteenth-century thought. This is true of many pedagogic conventions and traditions that we take for granted, but it is also true of the idealism that still animates our belief in education. Matthew Arnold, a major poet and also a professional educationalist, was among the most eloquent of those who argued for schooling of a kind that would amount to more than the means to economic advantage:

> Now, all the liberty and industry in the world will not ensure these two things: a high reason and a fine culture. They may favour them, but they will not of themselves produce them: they may exist without them. But it is by the appearance of these two things, in some shape or other, in the life of the nation, that it becomes something other than an independent, an energetic, a successful nation – that it becomes a *great* nation.[2]

In 1996, Tony Blair signalled the modernity of his policies with a celebrated mantra: 'Education, education, education'. Nothing could have sounded a more authentically Victorian note. Whatever else might define the values of the Victorians, their commitment to systematic learning was unshakeable. Throughout Britain and its imperial possessions, they worked to extend its reach. Schools were founded or renewed – ragged schools, elementary schools, public schools, girls' schools, board schools and night schools. In 1870, Forster's Education Act laid the foundations of a system that would provide free and compulsory education for all children, funded, as Arnold had wished, by the state. What we would now call institutions of higher education proliferated, from colleges for the godless or the commercial in London and elsewhere, to the new civic universities in the industrial cities of the Midlands and North. Mechanics' Institutes, local colleges and the University Extension Movement made education beyond the most basic level available to a much larger proportion of the population in 1900 than in 1837, when Victoria came to the throne. For the first time, significant numbers of British women had access to education at a serious and ambitious level. The Civil Service Reform Act of 1871 meant that competitive examination, rather than social connection, began to control access to influential posts in public administration. These were developments that amounted to a revolution, and they made the creation of a modern industrial society in Britain possible.[3]

Like most revolutions, this one was driven by divided and sometimes incompatible aspirations. Changing balances of power in social class, religious authority, gender and national identity meant that reformers' motives were often distorted by concerns that had no part in the first impulse to act. One of the purposes of this book is to show how varieties of self-interest could intervene in the broader ambition to vitalize education. No matter how well-intentioned, Victorians found such partiality hard to recognize, and harder to contain – a problem that is not unfamiliar to our own educational policy-makers. Even Matthew Arnold, who worked tirelessly to make a richer education accessible to all children, was sometimes blind to the ways in which his advocation of the classical ideal (deeply rooted in his memories of his father Dr Thomas Arnold, the innovative headmaster of Rugby) might in practice restrict opportunities for working-class children, and especially for girls. Matthew Arnold's determination to expand education makes him representative of many social activists, though his contributions had more impact than most. But his principles were coloured by a very personal understanding of education, and here too he was characteristic of his generation. The Victorians transformed educational practice, but there was no generally agreed theoretical basis for their numerous plans for reform. Through political battles at local and national levels, vigorous arguments conducted in books and periodicals, religious altercations and campaigns to establish or modernize educational institutions, the Victorians never stopped debating the nature of good education and the right way to achieve it. The most far-reaching among the shifts in cultural authority that lay behind this push was the changing status of religion, as the dominance of the churches retreated before the pressures of science, scholarship and social change. Many of the controversies that I shall discuss were driven by anxiety about how far, if at all, education might take on the spiritual and imaginative work of faith, a question that we have not yet succeeded in answering. Quarrelling about educational principles and policy can feel like a peculiarly modern preoccupation, but our problems remain stubbornly close to those that worried our predecessors.

Conflicts in Learning

The essential lines of opposition in matters of education are sharply articulated by the novelists, poets, historians and critics of the period, and it is through their work that I shall explore the conflicts that gave these debates their urgency. Victorian writers of every description were intensely interested in education. This was partly because it had transformed their own professional prospects, for the rapid expansion and changing tastes of a literate book-buying public offered huge possibilities for writers. Some literary figures of real distinction, particularly towards the end of the nineteenth century, would never have become writers at all without these new educational possibilities. The influence of Owens College, Manchester, was crucial in George Gissing's development as a major novelist. The poet and novelist Amy Levy would not have made her mark without the help of Brighton High School for girls, followed by Newnham College, in Cambridge, where she was the first Jewish woman to be admitted. Openings like these brought responsibilities. Should it be the business of writers to engage with matters of educational policy? Many thought that it should, and lively discussions about schooling figure in their works. But a still more fundamental doubt lay beneath this interest. Should literature, like religion or charity, take its own share in the work of teaching? And if so, what could it teach?

It was not uncommon for writers to have professional or institutional links with the work of education. But the culture of pedagogy was so prevalent that those with no such associations were often just as concerned with its potential. Tacitly sensed, or explicitly argued, the feeling grew that some measure of didactic purpose was a necessary part of an author's calling. In his brisk *Autobiography* (1883), looking back on an extraordinarily successful career as a novelist, Anthony Trollope is candid about the futility of the years he had spent at élite public schools (Harrow, Winchester) in the 1820s and early 1830s. The chief result of his own education had been to make him unhappy. But he insists that a novelist cannot avoid combining the need to give pleasure with the duties of a moral teacher – or, perhaps more surprisingly, a preacher:

> The writer of stories must please, or he will be nothing. And he must teach whether he wish to teach or no. How shall he teach lessons of virtue and at the same time make himself a delight to his readers? That sermons are not in themselves often thought to be agreeable we all know. Nor are disquisitions on moral philosophy supposed to be pleasant light reading for our idle hours. But the novelist, if he have a conscience, must preach his sermons with the same purpose as the clergyman, and must have his own system of ethics.[4]

Few would have chosen to point to the parallel with Trollope's characteristic bluntness. It is not easy to think of the worldly

Thackeray picturing himself as a sermonizer. Yet Trollope's view of the 'high nature of the work'[5] was widely shared among writers of the period. This might seem simply the expression of a bid for respectability, and no doubt the wish to claim gentility had some part to play in such sentiments. Writers wanted to be seen as gentlemen, and ladies, and their work as paid entertainers made that identity precarious. This was particularly true for novelists, whose efforts were often seen as a shade vulgar beside the loftier productions of poets. But the roots of this aim lay deeper than an inclination to assert authorial dignity. Trollope's specific reference to 'the clergyman' is telling. If the church could no longer instruct and improve the population – and little in Trollope's ecclesiastical novels suggests that he believed that it could – then perhaps literature should assume some of those duties. And if religion was no longer up to the task, writers must seek another 'system of ethics'.

This is different from fiction's potential use in the transmission of factual knowledge, or to promote a political or social campaign, though some writers also attempt these roles. Trollope wants to teach the principles of moral discrimination, founded in the experience of his readers. His autobiography makes the point directly:

> I have ever thought of myself as a preacher of sermons, and my pulpit as one which I could make both salutary and agreeable to my audience. I do believe that no girl has risen from the reading of my pages less modest than she was before, and that some may have learned from them that modesty is a charm well worth preserving. I think that no youth has been taught that in falseness and flashness is to be found the road to manliness; but some may perhaps have learned from me that it is to be found in truth and a high but gentle spirit. Such are the lessons I have striven to teach; and I have thought it might best be done by representing to my readers characters like themselves, – or to which they might liken themselves.[6]

Trollope's argument turns on the interiority of fiction. His quiet domestic stories offered readers a fictional mirror, in which they could see heightened versions of their own lives. Novels might help towards a fuller self-awareness, and perhaps also to better behaviour, within the clear-cut terms of what Trollope defines as good conduct. But this is necessarily a precarious exchange of values. No novelist, no matter how fastidious, can dictate the responses of the reader, who will sometimes be obstinately inclined to prefer flashiness to the charms of modesty. Worse still, the writer's own sympathies might ally themselves with the irresponsible and unworthy. For all the devout hopes of his autobiography, Trollope's work generates ambiguities that cannot be contained within the simple codes he describes. He must depend on a fluid reciprocity of the imagination, animating the moral intelligence of his readers. It is a creative response, not a passive one, drawing on the reader's own contribution. The ways in which this might work are unenforceable. The process readily backfires, and will sometimes fail entirely.

This difficulty leads to a point that I want to emphasize, for it lies behind many of the dilemmas that shape educational policies. The kind of teaching that Trollope's fiction offers cannot be regulated, or examined. Its outcomes are unpredictable. It is tempting, therefore, to think that it can play no real part in education. Perhaps it would be better to define schooling as the transmission of solid information, or knowledge – which can be seen as disinterested and communal, not personal and solitary. This is safer ground. After all, the impartiality of knowledge can also be seen as a moral asset. Its solid disciplines guard against the indulgences of invention, or the seductions of uncontrolled emotion. It can be objectively measured. If education is to be funded from the national purse, then it must be accountable, and formal and open examination is surely the only just way of assessing its efficiency. As more public money was invested in schools, this became an influential line of argument. Robert Lowe, as Vice-President of the Education Department, was primarily responsible for the introduction of the Revised Code in 1862, which provided for a carefully prescribed annual examination in schools funded by the state: '... we are about to substitute for the vague and indefinite test which now exists, a definite, clear, and precise test, so that the public may know exactly what consideration they get for their money.'[7]

There is a laudable clarity of intention in Lowe's position, and such thinking is a useful safeguard against the hazards of wasted public resources. Information, and the assessment of its acquisition, is essential to any large-scale educational system funded from general taxation, and will remain so. But the economic argument can become repressive, if its ascendancy is so complete and exclusive that it leaves no room for less readily testable forms of mental development. For all their indeterminacy, these different kinds of growth are also indispensable, in personal and social terms. Fiction can highlight some of the differences in perception that are key to these debates. The unassuming loyalty of Esther Summerson in Charles Dickens's *Bleak House* (1853), or Johnny Eames in Anthony Trollope's *The Small House at Allington* (1864), or Dorothea Brooke in George Eliot's *Middlemarch* (1871–2) is tried by suffering, compromised by circumstances, and finally rewarded with maturity. Their perplexities, and the uncertainty of our response, are inseparable from the kind of fictional education that Trollope describes. For all Dickens's labours on her behalf, plenty of readers find nothing more than priggishness in Esther Summerson's modest goodness. Dorothea Brooke's self-effacing story is a disappointment to many, while Johnny Eames's dogged devotion strikes others as simply ridiculous. We can learn from these characters, or we can find them tiresome: it is up to us, and our reaction is not to be measured against a fixed yardstick of correctness. The novelist takes the risk, and the result cannot be guaranteed. The educative potential of such figures depends on the fact that they are not exceptional or glamorous. Nor are they especially clever. They recall the untold numbers evoked by George Eliot, in the closing words of *Middlemarch*, of those 'who lived faithfully a hidden life'. Dorothea's unobtrusive influence is not to be dismissed simply because it cannot be counted, being 'incalculably diffusive'.[8] We might, as Trollope claimed, see a finer version of ourselves in such subdued histories. These provide fictional models that can be rewardingly studied. Not every such text will be a Victorian domestic novel: poetry, science fiction, fantasy, drama, adventure stories, travel writing, biographies and autobiographies – they all have their distinctive contribution to make. The value of reading and producing what is oddly called 'creative writing' (as if all writing were not creative) is part of the case I want to make here. But this is not the whole point. What I want to suggest is that these works remind us that worthwhile knowledge is not always a matter for impersonal certainty. Schools, colleges and universities are necessarily central to teaching we offer our children and young people. But we must acknowledge that quantifiable outcomes cannot be the only end of education, or the process of measurement will stifle the balanced expansion and growth that it is designed to assess.

This is not simply an intellectual dilemma. It has practical consequences, as the Victorians were aware. Learning that can be readily tested assumes a disproportionate significance if it becomes the primary route to the qualifications which allow entry to secure employment. In the satirical novel *Gryll Grange* (1860), Thomas Love Peacock's acerbic Doctor Opimian is scathing on the relentless spread of competitive examinations:

> I saw the other day some examination papers which would have infallibly excluded Marlborough from the army and Nelson from the navy. I doubt if Haydn would have passed as a composer before a committee of lords like one of his pupils, who insisted on demonstrating to him that he was continually sinning against the rules of counterpoint; on which Haydn said to him, 'I thought I was to teach you, but it seems you are to teach me, and I do not want a preceptor,' and thereon he wished his lordship a good morning ... Ask a candidate for a clerkship what are his qualifications? He may answer, 'All that are requisite – reading, writing, and arithmetic.' 'Nonsense,' says the questioner. 'Do you know the number of miles in direct distance from Timbuctoo to the top of Chimborazo?' 'I do not,' says the candidate. 'Then you will not do for a clerk,' says the competitive examiner.[9]

For all their egalitarian virtues, national systems of examination worried many Victorian observers. If knowledge becomes nothing more than a pile of unconnected facts, its liberating potential will be lost. Matthew Arnold, with many years as an inspector of schools behind him, asks his readers to consider the possibility that 'of education what is called *information* is really the least part.'[10]

These divergences were widely debated. The primacy of information as the basis for education was both a reassurance and a threat, especially for those brought up as confident Christians. As the intellectual authority of theology faltered, there was a commonly felt need for evolving forms of faith that might take its place. Writers were divided in their reaction, often forthright in their support for the expansion of education, but voicing uneasiness at what might be excluded from knowledge-based models for learning. This was as true for poets as it was for novelists. Alfred Tennyson, with his unfailing instinct for the issues that most troubled his audience, moved between the poles of cultural value represented by faith and knowledge throughout his long career. He was among those who believed that the extension of learning was both admirable and necessary. *The Princess* (1847), a poem which advocates the education of women, describes popular scientific instruction as it happens on the lawn of a stately home:

> There moved the multitude, a thousand heads:
> The patient leaders of their Institute
> Taught them with facts.[11]

Tennyson approves of this work, but the poetry persistently withdraws from it. In fact his refusal is more absolute than anything we might find in Trollope or George Eliot, for it denies the claims of social obligation of any kind. The resolute good sense of *The Princess* is undercut by the irresponsibilities of feeling, creating a strange dissonance of grief within what could be described as Tennyson's most politically engaged poem, and certainly the poem most specifically concerned with the benefits of education:

> Tears, idle tears, I know not what they mean,
> Tears from the depth of some divine despair

10

> Rise in the heart, and gather to the eyes,
> In looking on the happy Autumn-fields,
> And thinking of the days that are no more.[12]

This pensive lyric in the midst of *The Princess* is disquietingly distant from any celebration of knowledge, but it is just as far from any history of feeling that could possibly serve as a basis for teaching. Tears are subject to neither logic nor investigation. 'I know not what they mean', says Tennyson, and this is the source of their authority.

Three years later, Tennyson's *In Memoriam,* the long and ambitious elegy which in 1850 served as his qualification to become the nation's Poet Laureate, broods on these difficulties. It affirms the transcendence of faith, though its definitions of what that might mean are always tentative and elusive. But it also honours the expansion of knowledge, in a double assertion of value carried on eddying currents of thought:

> We have but faith: we cannot know;
> For knowledge is of things we see;
> And yet we trust it comes from thee,
> A beam in darkness: let it grow.[13]

Most of Tennyson's readers, anxious to commend enlightened learning without conceding any corresponding danger to religion, would have agreed. Nevertheless, the growing influence of knowledge can seem menacing as we encounter it in his work. For all its potential benefits, it might become a destructive power. Tennyson wants to keep it in its place. *In Memoriam* is outspoken on the matter:

> Who loves not Knowledge? Who shall rail
> Against her beauty? May she mix
> With men and prosper! Who shall fix
> Her pillars? Let her work prevail.
>
> But on her forehead sits a fire:
> She sets her forward countenance

11

And leaps into the future chance,
Submitting all things to desire.

Half-grown as yet, a child, and vain –
She cannot fight the fear of death.
What is she, cut from love and faith,
But some wild Pallas from the brain

Of Demons? fiery-hot to burst
All barriers in her onward race
For power. Let her know her place;
She is the second, not the first.[14]

Knowledge is seen in these stanzas as petulantly immature – a selfish child, badly in need of teaching, rather than the reliably useful product of education. This is a startling outburst, with its suggestion that knowledge might become demonic, driven by desire and a burning hunger for domination. Described in this way, it has lost the virtues of cool impartiality. It is all too emotional, driven by wilful passion. Tennyson's language here is provocative, but it formulates an anxiety that shadowed the minds of many Victorians, both those who taught and those who learned. The spread of education founded on knowledge was welcomed, but the applause was qualified by a sense that its triumph might bring costs alongside benefits. Other values might be lost, harder to identify or quantify, but necessary.

Poetry and Teaching: William Wordsworth

The fear that the wrong kind of learning might destroy the right kind of feeling was not invented by the Victorians. It can be identified as one of the most durable strands in British Romantic thought, and at this point I want to consider some of its more significant points of origin. William Wordsworth is a seminal presence here, as he often is in the thinking that bridges Romantic and Victorian culture.[15] Commonly identified as a teacher, he was nevertheless hostile to the idea that his writing could in any straightforward sense be an advocation of what can be learned from books. The lessons that he tells us matter most are not to be found in schools, or even within the bounds of language itself.

Wordsworth contemplated the problem in the 'Reply to "Mathetes"', published in *The Friend* in 1809. 'Mathetes'[16] had asked Wordsworth to identify himself as a teacher for his generation, a reassuring source of authority who would protect the 'youthful spirit' from the consequences of rash enthusiasm:

> Here then is the power of delusion that will gather round the first steps of a youthful spirit, and throw enchantment over the world in which it is to dwell. – Hope realizing its own dreams: – Ignorance dazzled and ravished with sudden sunshine: – Power awakened and rejoicing in its own consciousness: – Enthusiasm kindling among multiplying images of greatness and beauty ... Now as this delusion springs not from his worse but his better nature, it seems as if there could be no warning to him from within of his own danger.[17]

Such a spirit needed the 'living Teacher' from outside. That teacher was to be Wordsworth, whose name calls up to many 'the recollection of their weakness, and the consciousness of their strength'.[18] But in his reply Wordsworth explicitly refuses to become a moral teacher, explaining that learning gained in that way will not provide what is really needed. What he has to teach is that Mathetes must do without teaching, if the knowledge he acquires is to be alive:

> There is a life and spirit in knowledge which we extract from truths scattered for the benefit of all, and which the mind, by its own activity, has appropriated to itself – a life and a spirit, which is seldom found in knowledge communicated by formal and direct precepts, even when they are exalted and endeared by reverence and love for the Teacher.[19]

The way to the actively realized knowledge that Wordsworth values must be circuitous and uncharted, and it will involve the individual comprehension of mistakes, for there can 'be no confirmed and passionate love of truth for him who has not experienced the hollowness of error.'[20] In this sense, no teacher can protect or even guide the developing mind, for each must take his own hard road:

> Nature has irrevocably decreed that our prime dependence in all stages of life after Infancy and Childhood have been passed through (nor do I know that this latter ought to be excepted) must be upon our own minds; and that the way to knowledge shall be long, difficult, winding, and often times returning upon itself.[21]

A sense of a fruitful return is a recurrent motif in the writing of those who reflect on these issues in terms of the living connection with the past that history or memory might allow.

For Wordsworth, this is not always a matter of simply learning from the past – sometimes it is a helpless repetition, an uncanny haunting from which others may learn, but not those who have been unable to escape their own histories. Martha Ray, the betrayed mother in Wordsworth's radical poem 'The Thorn', published in *Lyrical Ballads* (1798), has only one thing to say, and her repeated cry is neither beautiful nor intellectually distinguished:

> Oh misery! Oh misery!
> Oh woe is me! Oh misery![22]

In his 'Note to "The Thorn"', published in 1800, Wordsworth justifies his position:

> Words, a Poet's words more particularly, ought to be weighed in the balance of feeling, and not measured by the space which they occupy upon paper. For the Reader cannot be too often reminded that Poetry is passion: it is the history or science of feelings: now every man must know that an attempt is rarely made to communicate impassioned feelings without something of an accompanying sense of the inadequateness of our own powers, or the deficiencies of language. During such efforts there will be a craving in the mind, and as long as it is

14

unsatisfied the Speaker will cling to the same words, or words of the same character. There are also various other reasons why repetition and apparent tautology are frequent beauties of the highest kind. Among the chief of these reasons is the interest which the mind attaches to words, not only as symbols of the passions, but as *things*, active and efficient, which are of themselves part of the passion. And further, from a spirit of fondness, exultation, and gratitude, the mind luxuriates in the repetition of words which appear successfully to communicate its feelings.[23]

The expression or communication of knowledge is a very long way from the point of poetry as Wordsworth conceives it in this odd and challenging note. The real business of poetry is not with reason, nor beauty, but with emotion – 'passion, or the history or science of feelings'. Repetition may be the most potent means of conveying the intensity of feeling that Wordsworth claims as the purpose of the poet. The logical power of language falls away in the face of the disturbing inner pressures that impel poetry and its readers. Deprived of the intellectual substance of language, we grow attached to the consoling material of the words themselves – not as abstract signs but, in Wordsworth's definition here, '*things, active and efficient*'. The words 'thing', or 'something', recur repeatedly in Wordsworth's early poetry at moments of its greatest intensity, as he withdraws from what writing can do in the presence of 'something' greater than writing, beyond the definitions of thought. Such moments are likely to be associated with the passive suffering of those who are excluded from fully articulate speech, because they are poor, or very old, or very young, or because their lives have driven them, like Martha Ray, to the edges of a human community. The reader might learn from Martha, but Wordsworth does not make a teacher of her.

Such convictions did not prevent Wordsworth from writing pro-lifically and often didactically throughout his long life as a poet. But they did prompt him to qualify his teaching with repeated denials that the exercise of didacticism can have any lasting authority. This is an insistent element in the thinking of *Lyrical Ballads*, where Wordsworth's advocation of the educational energy of feeling rather

15

than the authority of textual knowledge takes an especially uncompromising form. The old Cumberland beggar, the most ignorant of all his lonely travellers, and the most in want, is another provocative example of what Wordsworth defines as the redemptive power of suffering. The beggar's repeated circuits as a traveller, supported by the charity of the households who know him, seem to be a peculiarly bleak expression of the 'way to knowledge' – 'long, difficult, winding, and often times returning upon itself'. Yet Wordsworth defiantly claims that the intellectual and physical destitution that this inarticulate beggar represents might be seen as the true source of the moral energy of poets, or even of his own poetry. The insight that distinguishes poets,

> lofty minds
> And meditative, authors of delight
> And happiness,[24]

derives from those, like the beggar, who have not themselves been instructed, and are perhaps incapable of instruction:

> ... from this solitary being
> This helpless wanderer, have perchance received,
> (A thing more precious far than all that books
> Or the solicitudes of love can do!)
> That first mild touch of sympathy and thought,
> In which they found their kindred with a world
> Where want and sorrow were.[25]

Like many of the poems of the *Lyrical Ballads,* this states an extreme position. The learning that matters to poets has to do with sympathy. It is kindred with want and sorrow, rather than with formal learning – 'all that books ... can do' – or even, Wordsworth suggests, personal affection – 'the solicitudes of love'. The returning presence of the pitiful beggar is a remembered obligation, a lesson beyond anything that can be written, though we encounter it in a written text. Its implications are not limited to poets, or those who are characterized

16

by any exceptional capacity for a high purpose. It reaches 'yet further',[26] as Wordsworth tells us. The habit of giving compelled by the beggar's absolute need expands the humanity of the poor, not just the rich, or the literate:

> ... man is dear to man; the poorest poor
> Long for some moments in a weary life
> When they can know and feel that they have been
> Themselves the fathers and the dealers out
> Of some small blessings, have been kind to such
> As needed kindness, for this single cause,
> That we have all of us one human heart.[27]

These are poems that challenge the easy assumption of those who habitually read poetry: 'Gentlemen, persons of fortune, professional men, ladies, persons who can afford to buy or can easily procure books', as Wordsworth describes them, are inclined to believe that 'human nature and the persons they associate with are one and the same thing'.[28] The lessons of the *Lyrical Ballads* insist on a common humanity, rather than creating or reinforcing distinctions between the prosperously literate and the impoverished and untaught. Wordsworth's point has to do with a community of feeling, but his unsettling argument also has a measured political force.

The culmination of these recurrent moments in *Lyrical Ballads* is located at the heart of Wordsworth's 'Lines Written a Few Miles Above Tintern Abbey', where this most sophisticated and articulate of the collection's poems withdraws into the resistant indefinition of its great climax:

> And I have felt
> A presence that disturbs me with the joy
> Of elevated thoughts; a sense sublime
> Of something far more deeply interfused,
> Whose dwelling is the light of setting suns,
> And the round ocean, and the living air,
> And the blue sky, and in the mind of man,

17

> A motion and a spirit, that impels
> All thinking things, all objects of all thought,
> And rolls through all things.[29]

Here the collapse of language becomes its triumph. The poet can only gesture towards experience of a kind that poetry cannot touch. Yet such experience remains, as Wordsworth understands it, the true concern of poetry. Wordsworth's writing moves beyond rational argument, or literary debate. 'A motion and a spirit, that impels/All thinking things, all objects of all thought,/And rolls through all things' – what does it mean? In one sense, it means nothing. But its repudiation of exactitude gives this poetry a comprehensive emotional intensity that haunted Wordsworth's Victorian successors.

Wordsworth's example defines an aesthetic that rests on the education of feeling, rather than the transmission of fact. His close association with the landscape of the Lake District added a further dimension to his authority, suggesting that the authenticity of emotion could be identified with a natural environment, distinct from the contaminations of industrial urbanization. Many saw Wordsworth in vague terms as the unassailable advocate of the priority of the imagination; others were more precise in their acknowledgement of his power. In his *Autobiography* (1873), John Stuart Mill describes the youthful depression from which his sophisticated powers of analysis could not retrieve him, for it was a paralysis of feeling that had stopped his life in its tracks, rather than an intellectual crisis. His extraordinarily ambitious and wide-ranging education had resulted in alienation, from his friends and from himself. Reading Wordsworth revived him:

> What made Wordsworth's poems a medicine for my state of mind, was that they expressed, not mere outward beauty, but states of feeling, and of thought coloured by feeling, under the excitement of beauty. They seemed to be the very culture of the feelings, which I was in quest of. In them I seemed to draw from a source of inward joy, of sympathetic and imaginative pleasure, which could be shared in by all human beings.[30]

18

Mill, who knew himself to be truly exceptional, felt that he had been rescued from despair by Wordsworth's reminder that he was also like other men, 'for we have all of us one human heart'. He points out that such perspectives were not incompatible with the knowledge on which his philosophy was built, for

> the imaginative emotion which an idea, when vividly conceived, excites in us, is not an illusion but a fact, as real as any of the other qualities of objects; and far from implying anything erroneous and delusive in our mental apprehension of the object, is quite consistent with the most accurate knowledge and most perfect practical recognition of all its physical and intellectual laws and relations. The intensest feeling of the beauty of a cloud lighted by the setting sun, is no hindrance to my knowing that the cloud is vapour of water, subject to all the laws of vapours in a state of suspension; and I am just as likely to allow for, and act on, these physical laws whenever there is occasion to do so, as if I had been incapable of perceiving any distinction between beauty and ugliness.[31]

But he had come to believe that the reality of active understanding must include the imaginative emotion that Wordsworth had authorized for him. In this he was representative of many Victorians in their effort to incorporate all that Wordsworth stood for within the subsequent development of education and letters.

Imagination and Fact

Deeply influenced by their Romantic predecessors but often uncertain about the consequences of that legacy, the Victorians were preoccupied by the point of conjunction between the private energies of the imagination and the public standing of verifiable fact. This difficult association was seen to be as crucial to the disciplines of the historian as to the scientist, philosopher or novelist. Victorian thinkers came to think of themselves as the products of history, in what John Stuart Mill defined as the 'dominant idea' of the age.[32]

History was no fantasy, but the product of reality. Thomas Carlyle, whose intellectual energies as a historian defined many of the terms of these arguments for those who came after him, was famously scornful of the claims of poetry, or fiction, beside those of solid reality. The work that established his reputation, *The French Revolution* (1837), declares its grand narrative to be immovably grounded in actuality. 'For life is no cunningly-devised deception or self-deception: it is a great truth that thou art alive, that thou hast desires, necessities; neither can these subsist and satisfy themselves on delusions, but on fact.'[33] And yet historical fact was never quite enough in itself, for only the resources of the imagination, delusory or not, could represent its densities. The men and women who were the subjects of historical study had evidently not been animated by facts alone, and their lives could not be fully understood without some acknowledgement of the passions that had motivated them. Carlyle's historical writing is vividly Romantic, and draws heavily and persistently on the strategies of literature. In his 'Thoughts on History', he sees the matter as predominantly one of formal method. The historian must find a way of embracing events that were not simply '*successive*', as a simple linear chronicle might suggest, but '*simultaneous*'.[34] In order to unpick the interwoven substance of the past, the historian must make connections and suggest patterns of causality and consequence. The representation of fact is expanded into the nuance of fiction. Readers are drawn into the life of the past through a cluster of images, for the simultaneity of what the eye perceives can qualify the linear succession of a simple historical narrative. Carlyle is strikingly visual in his methods as a historian. For him, as for Tennyson, 'knowledge is of things we see'.

In *Past and Present* (1843), Carlyle's clearest statement of historical method, its visual elements are repeatedly asserted: ' "House and people, royal and episcopal, lord and varlets, where are they?" "Why *there*, I say, Seven Centuries off; sunk *so* far in the Night, there they *are*; peep through the blankets of old Night, and thou wilt see!" '[35] This visuality is finally a work of the imagination, for the study of history might be best understood as looking into 'a pair of eyes deep as our own, *imaging* our own'.[36] Fact – 'pure, crude fact' as Robert Browning was to call it, 'secreted from man's life' – could only be fully formed and realized in the mind's eye.[37] The historian J. A. Froude, Carlyle's most influential and popular follower and later his biographer, understood the ruptures in Carlyle's position, and knew that they were productive. The eye is a creative organ, and it does not imagine as the camera records. Writing in 1854, Froude concedes that it 'is not questioned that if we *could* arrive at a *full daguerrotyped objective* account of things, such an account would be of profit to us'. But this is neither possible, nor altogether to be wished, for the most rigorous depictions of historical fact 'must first be alloyed with fiction'.[38] Like Carlyle, Froude gave his readers versions of historical narrative that shared some of the developing sophistication of the novel, the form that dominated the literary landscapes of the nineteenth century. History could teach, and both Carlyle and his interpreter Froude intended that it should. But the work could not be done without the reciprocation of creative vision. This was a fertile dynamic, but for historians as for novelists and poets it could also be a troublesome one.

Such concerns were not confined to British culture. Many of the most sharply felt controversies were bound up with consonant developments in Continental thought, which were also responsive to educational change. Revisionary theories of history were perhaps the most pervasive of the stream of German ideas that energized the intellectual life of nineteenth-century Britain. They reached a high level of intensity in the work of Friedrich Nietzsche. His early essay 'On the Uses and Disadvantages of History for Life' (1874), published in *Untimely Meditations* (1873–6), confronts the issues directly. Though the essay was not widely read in Britain on first publication, its preoccupations reiterate some of those that I have been discussing in British thinking of the period. Debating legacies of German Romanticism that became a potent presence in Victorian educational strategies, Nietzsche characteristically identifies the culture of knowledge with the culture of historicism. Nietzsche is not inclined to underestimate what history can do for us. But he is certain that it cannot do everything. Before historical knowledge can be truly useful, it must be more than a matter of a body of information, acquired as a means of insulating the self from its own needs. It must connect the imagination with the world, as an inward resource that will express itself in action, and allow for growth.

In the foreword to his essay, Nietzsche begins with a quotation from Goethe:

> 'In any case, I hate everything that merely instructs me without augmenting or directly invigorating my activity.' These words are from Goethe, and they may stand as a sincere *ceterum censeo*,[39] at the beginning of our meditation on the value of history. For its intention is to show why instruction without invigoration, why knowledge not attended by action, why history as a costly superfluity and luxury, must, to use Goethe's word, be seriously hated by us – hated because we still lack even the things we need and the superfluous is the enemy of the necessary. We need history, certainly but we need it for reasons different from those for which the idler in the garden of knowledge needs it, even though he may look nobly down on our rough and charmless needs and requirements. We need it, that is to say, for the sake of life and action, not so as to turn comfortably away from life and action, let alone for the purpose of extenuating the self-seeking life and the base and cowardly action. We want to serve history only to the extent that history serves life.[40]

Historical knowledge is necessary, but it is not the only necessity. Wrongly characterized, it could also be the enemy of what Nietzsche elsewhere in this essay calls 'a sound and whole inwardness'.[41] It could replace living intelligence with dead material. This, in Nietzsche's argument, was the process that had paralysed education for his generation:

> Examine with this in mind the literature of our higher school and educational system over the past decades: one will see with angry astonishment that, all the varying proposals and vehement contentions notwithstanding, the actual objective of education is everywhere

thought of as being the same; that the outcome of education hitherto, the production of the 'educated man' as he is at present understood, is unhesitatingly assumed to be the necessary and rational foundation of all future education. The uniform canon is that the young man has to start with a knowledge of culture, not even with a knowledge of life and even less with life and experience itself ... His desire to experience something himself and to feel evolving within him a coherent living complex of experiences of his own – such a desire is confused and as it were made drunk by the illusory promise that it is possible to sum up in oneself the highest and most noteworthy experiences of former ages, and precisely the greatest of former ages, in a few years.[42]

Nietzsche's position is provocative, but its grounds are clear. His argument represents the culmination of the anxieties about divisions between letter and spirit that shadow educational thought throughout the nineteenth century.

Poetry and Schooling: Matthew Arnold

Though they were more conciliatory than Nietzsche's stark interpretation of this conflict, the literary discourses of education that developed in the mid-Victorian period often struggle with internal splits of the kind that Wordsworth had described. Some found the political consequences of this divided ideology impossible to sustain. Matthew Arnold is an example of a poet who chose to renounce the attempt to hold such tensions together and instead devoted himself to the development of a liberal educational practice sponsored by the state. His poetry is deeply rooted in his close and extensive reading of Wordsworth, whose reputation had a peculiarly personal weight in his life, partly through his family's connections with the Lake District. For Arnold, the august older poet came to represent the unreachable confidence of his father's generation, a strength of understanding and purpose that could not be maintained in his own corrupted age. Arnold's poetry happens in dark and solitary places, beyond the reach of knowledge, and unconsoled by the sympathetic engagement with common feeling that had restored Mill's creativity. Unlike Wordsworth, Arnold hardly believes that the inner life can be reached at all:

> And long we try in vain to speak and act
> Our hidden self, and what we say and do
> Is eloquent, is well – but 'tis not true![43]

The memorial verses that Arnold wrote on Wordsworth's death in 1850 lament the loss of an earlier confident aesthetic of feeling, crushed by what had come to seem an enfeebled culture 'of doubts, disputes, distractions, fears'.[44] Wordsworth is described as the 'last poetic voice'.[45] No succession is possible. Instead, we are given a comfortless but obstinately explicit diagnosis of a modern disease. Arnold outlines the situation of his beleaguered age with unhappy relish:

> But where will Europe's latter hour
> Again find Wordsworth's healing power?
> Others will teach us how to dare,
> And against fear our breast to steel;
> Others will strengthen us to bear –
> But who, ah! who, will make us feel?[46]

Arnold's sense of estrangement from his own creativity found sombre expression in his 'Empedocles Upon Etna', where the tormented philosopher-hero's extended deliberations on the loss of life and freedom finally lead to self-immolation in the mouth of the volcano. In what feels like a particularly comprehensive enactment of Nietzsche's claim that annihilation is the final goal of knowledge, this forbidding poem contends that intellectual growth has come to seem a denial of life, rather than its affirmation. Empedocles's fragmentation is reflected in his language, as he turns on himself:

24

> But no, this heart will glow no more; thou art
> A living man no more, Empedocles!
> Nothing but a devouring flame of thought –
> But a naked, eternally restless mind![47]

Arnold's Empedocles gives the reader a peculiarly embittered and self-lacerating image of what a life of thought might amount to:

> I have lived in wrath and gloom,
> Fierce, disputatious, ever at war with man,
> Far from my own soul, far from warmth and light.[48]

Withdrawing this poem with a dramatic flourish from his 1853 collection, Arnold describes what had come to seem its disabling weakness. It could make no worthwhile contribution to knowledge:

> We all naturally take pleasure, says Aristotle, in any imitation or representation whatever: this is the basis of our love of poetry; and we take pleasure in them, he adds, because all knowledge is naturally agreeable to us; not to the philosopher only, but to mankind at large. Every representation therefore which is consistently drawn may be supposed to be interesting, inasmuch as it gratifies the natural interest in knowledge of all kinds. What is *not* interesting, is that which does not add to our knowledge of any kind; that which is vaguely conceived, and loosely drawn; a representation which is general, indeterminate, and faint, instead of being particular, precise, and firm.

'Empedocles on Etna' had failed, Arnold declares, because it had not been educational in the right way. It had not communicated the helpful knowledge that he identifies as the chief value of poetry. Poems which can give no 'enjoyment' are 'those in which the suffering finds no vent in action; in which a continuous state of mental distress is prolonged, unrelieved by incident, hope or resistance; in which there is everything to be endured, nothing to be done'.[49] This might seem close to what Wordsworth had described in *The Lyrical Ballads*. But Arnold had lost sight of Wordsworth's understanding of the unyielding strength which can derive from suffering. He identifies Empedocles as the voice of defeat, an ancient prefiguring of the rootless generation which could not rise to the challenge that Wordsworth had left behind. A mountain was not, for Arnold, an image of spiritual growth or even of sublimity, but a place of consuming self-destruction.

The family business of education offered an alternative to the futility of the contemporary 'darkling plain', ringing with the confusions of its 'ignorant armies'.[50] Not only did Matthew Arnold become one of the most influential educational theorists of the nineteenth century, as an inspector of schools he immersed himself in the day-to-day business of teaching and learning as it was supported and directed by the state. His dedication is located in the work of the classroom, and it amounted to more than a mundane substitute for the higher satisfactions of poetry. He found that the public activities of education could provide him with a rewarding place in the world. Arnold never underestimated the substance that a vocation could give to a life. But he was not just an effective public servant. He was committed to values that were more than simply practical. The imaginative needs of a faltering generation could be addressed through the literature of the past, as a way of tempering the distresses of the disordered modern mind. Though Arnold was compelled to abandon Wordsworth's sober conviction that the individual could be steadied and nourished by a repeated connection with the life of feeling, he did not renounce the Wordsworthian notion that the cultivated memory, returning to moments of insight, must be the foundation of education.

Such broad hopes meant that schooling had to allow room for something other than instruction. Arnold was impatient with mechanical methods like those introduced by Robert Lowe's 1862 Revised Code, in which the financial aid given to schools depended on the attainment of the pupils as determined by the examination of visiting state-appointed inspectors.[51] Such a system – 'payment by results', as it came to be called – could not allow for the moral and spiritual training that he thought should be the final goal of any educational institution. Arnold's protests, published in *Fraser's Magazine* in March 1862, were immediate and sharp. Like his fellow reformer James Kay-Shuttleworth, he felt that the new scheme was demeaning for teachers, pupils, and inspectors alike, reducing schools to the status of purely commercial or industrial establishments. It was a practice, he argued, that would turn 'the inspectors into a set of registering clerks, with a mass of minute details to tabulate, such a system as must, in Sir James Shuttleworth's words, "necessarily withdraw their attention from the religious and general instruction, and from the moral features of the school"'.[52]

Lowe's unrelenting plans, widely disliked on their introduction and later significantly moderated, were designed to quantify the literacy and numeracy produced by public money. In a modified form, their objectives have returned to our own debates on the management of education – yet another reminder of how our thinking on education moves in circles. Performance-related pay is a contemporary version of payment by results, and it too must rely on the constant assessment of teachers alongside their pupils. Comments from senior members of the teaching profession have echoed Lowe's views: 'Teachers cannot expect something for nothing. Poor performance cannot be subsidised. In future pay will be linked to performance at the individual class teacher level.'[53] Now, as in the nineteenth century, reformers' motives are honourable, for children's opportunities to learn may be damaged if teachers are apathetic. The propagation of literacy and numeracy matters. Arnold was fully aware of its importance, but he argued that it should be a starting-place for education, and not its final objective. Twenty years after his quarrel with Lowe, he defined the wider purposes of learning in 'Literature and Science', an address delivered to an American audience as a revised version of his Cambridge Rede lecture of 1882. Education should not simply equip the young with weapons for the Darwinian struggle for existence. Taking issue with T. H. Huxley's 'Science and Culture', a lecture given in Birmingham three years previously, Arnold denies that an education focused on what Huxley terms 'the stores of physical science' would be a sufficient basis for a

27

'criticism of life'.[54] On the other hand, a 'superficial humanism, mainly decorative' would be equally inadequate for the task.[55] Arnold is at his most engaging in his steadfast claims that education must satisfy both intellectual and imaginative needs. 'We experience, as we go on learning and knowing – the vast majority of us experience – the need of relating what we have learnt and known to the sense which we have in us for conduct, to the sense which we have in us for beauty.'[56] Knowledge of the material world cannot wholly satisfy these needs. His response echoes John Stuart Mill's remarks on watching a sunset. No matter how much we learn from scientists, no matter how useful such learning might be, 'still it will be *knowledge* only which they give us, knowledge not put for us into relation with our sense for conduct, our sense for beauty, and touched with emotion by being so put.'[57]

Arnold's turn of phrase here echoes the famous definition of religion in his *Literature and Dogma* (1873): 'The true meaning of religion is thus not simply *morality*, but *morality touched by emotion*'.[58] A measure of continuing internal division is revealed in the language: 'morality touched by emotion' suggests that morality and emotion are distinct and separate, rather than aspects of the same imaginatively apprehended whole. Yet it remained true, for Arnold, that knowledge or morality untouched by emotion cannot supply our deepest needs. Arnold's suspicion of the natural sciences, more clearly evident in 'Literature and Science' than in his earlier educational polemics, resolves itself in the feeling that the humanities will allow for a more engaged imaginative life, knowledge that could locate itself in the history of the emotions, and the desire for beauty.

> If then there is to be separation and option between humane letters on the one hand, and the natural sciences on the other, the great majority of mankind, all who have not exceptional and overpowering aptitudes for the study of nature, would do well, I cannot but think, to choose to be educated in humane letters rather than in the natural sciences. Letters will call out their being at more points, will make them live more.[59]

The central problem, as far as Arnold is concerned, was that the meanness of contemporary culture could not supply these emotional and imaginative needs. The hungry mind, eager to live more, must be fed by the literature of a better-regulated past, and especially by the wider horizons opened by the classical worlds of ancient Greece and Rome. The education to be found in the study of letters reaches its highest point where it began, in the 'high symmetry' of Greek culture. 'If the instinct for beauty is served by Greek literature and art as it is served by no other literature and art, we may trust to the instinct of self-preservation in humanity for keeping Greek as part of our culture. We may trust to it for even making the study of Greek more prevalent than it is now.'[60] Here Arnold's ambitious educational programme succumbs to wishful thinking. Classical civilization as he defines it could not represent a disinterested body of wisdom and beauty, equally accessible to all. It had also come to function as the mark of a scholar and a gentleman, and at this point Arnold's aspirations are caught in the snares of social divisions.

Despite Arnold's hope that 'women will again study Greek, as lady Jane Grey did',[61] it was clear that the traditions of nineteenth-century England meant that there could never be any prospect that a classical education would be widely accessible to women, even if they were to choose to apply themselves to the study of classical literature in large numbers, which was not probable. It was also unlikely that anything other than a minority of working men would become competent classical scholars, or indeed that many would rush to master Greek and Latin, if tuition were made available. Such study would have meant more than the contention with practical difficulties. It would have entailed a transformation of identity, of a kind that was never going to be universally feasible, or attractive. Few girls or labourers would choose to acquire the accomplishments of middle-class male gentility. The study of science, seen by Arnold as a distinctly second-rate pursuit, was more readily within the social compass of ambitious working-class students. It is equally true that contemporary literature, particularly fiction, was more likely to be attractive to women or working men than the classics, or even those

English authors (like Milton) whose work grew directly out of the classical tradition. Arnold's dismissal of the study of natural science, as he belittlingly quotes Darwin's 'famous proposition that "our ancestor was a hairy quadruped furnished with a tail and pointed ears, probably arboreal in his habits"',[62] makes depressing reading now. So too does his indifference to fiction by women, together with his unstated assumption that the ambitions of girls will be secondary to those of men.

The real limitation of Arnold's position lies in his insistence that the intellectual freedom that literature could provide was largely confined to the poetry of the past, particularly the classical past, and more particularly still the Hellenic past. Recent poetry and fiction could not measure up. Neither women nor industrial working populations could easily locate themselves within that strand of a grandly retrospective tradition. What Arnold wants to present as a universal experience was in practice socially exclusive, and it was bound up with the hierarchical structures of status implied in the identities of gender and class. Sydney Smith, among many others, had long since made the point: 'Classical quotations are the watchwords of scholars, by which they distinguish each other from the ignorant and illiterate; and Greek and Latin are insensibly become almost the only test of a cultivated mind.'[63] Despite his extensive work in schools throughout the country, which fired him with a genuine wish to make education a matter of imaginative liberation, Matthew Arnold's concept of education loses some of the comprehensive reach that had characterized Wordsworth's position.

Fiction and Memory: Charles Dickens

Charles Dickens, with his popular appeal, his confidence in the energies of fiction and his suspicion of the social complacencies that sometimes characterized Matthew Arnold's thought, might seem to be Arnold's natural opponent. Arnold thought Dickens irredeemably vulgar; Dickens had no time for Arnold's cool classicism. Nevertheless, they have much in common. They shared an unshakeable conviction that education could transform the lives of the poor, and create a richer and more generous nation. Both were uneasy about the public regulation of its energies, and neither was content to see the teaching of children confine itself to matters of fact. Disquiet about the role of public education bit deeply into the mind of Charles Dickens, the novelist whose work defined and to some extent initiated many of the changing directions of the period's literature. There is a moment that every reader remembers towards the end of *A Christmas Carol*, a hugely popular story that focuses many of the concerns of Dickens's early fiction with particular force. The newly chastened Scrooge is shown two dreadful phantoms by the Ghost of Christmas Present – 'yellow, meagre, ragged, scowling, wolfish'.[64] The Ghost explains who they are. 'This boy is Ignorance. This girl is Want. Beware them both, and all of their degree, but most of all beware this boy, for on his brow I see that written which is Doom, unless the writing be erased.'[65] Erasing the fatal writing on the brow of Ignorance is a persistent aspiration in Dickens's work, and it is one of the concerns that marks his voice as one of those that characterize the period. *A Christmas Carol* appeared in 1843, a moment when political and economic instability meant that alarm about the potentially disastrous consequences of ignorance was beginning to run high. Dickens was among those who were urging the expansion of education as the most effective safeguard against insurrection. In 1844, he made a rousing speech in Birmingham: 'If you would reward honesty, if you would give encouragement to good, if you would stimulate the idle, eradicate evil, or correct what is bad, education – comprehensive liberal education – is the one thing needful, and the one effective end.'[66] There was nothing ambivalent in such views, and certainly nothing indecisive. And yet the processes of education made Dickens uncomfortable. It is characteristic of his doubleness that the ghost's portentous prophecy should speak about education in terms of erasing writing, as though writing, the product of education, were also part of the problem. The erasure of writing is in fact a persistent preoccupation in *A Christmas Carol*. The climactic moment of the story might

31

be identified in Scrooge's agonized desire to 'sponge away' the words 'Ebenezer Scrooge' from the tombstone revealed by the Ghost of Christmas Yet to Come,[67] while the name of the condemned Jacob Marley is 'never painted out'.[68]

The 'needful' education that Scrooge profits from in *A Christmas Carol* is theatrical, almost cinematic – a matter of image and emotion, rather than textual instruction. Scrooge must enter fully into the lessons of his own past, which is what the first of the visiting spirits has to teach him. His memories must be internalized, felt and seen, and not simply a source of instruction and record. Scrooge's schooling, like almost every other process of formal education described in Dickens's fiction, had been alienating. He had been taught in the dismal surroundings that Dickens habitually associates with schools, in 'a mansion of dull red brick', its rooms 'poorly furnished, cold, and vast'.[69] Taken by the phantom to revisit the dreary old form-room, Scrooge is led into the restorative recesses of his own frozen memories.

> They went, the Ghost and Scrooge, across the hall, to a door in the back of the house. It opened before them, and disclosed a long, bare melancholy room, made barer still by lines of plain deal forms and desks. At one of these a lonely boy was reading near a feeble fire; and Scrooge sat down upon a form, and wept to see his poor forgotten self as he used to be.
>
> Not a latent echo in the house ... but fell upon the heart of Scrooge with a softening influence, and gave a freer passage to his tears.[70]

These tears, freed by 'thinking of the days that are no more', are not associated with memories of the instruction that made an effective businessman of Scrooge, but with images of the vivid characters conjured by his solitary childhood reading. For Dickens, as for Carlyle, education is a matter of vision:

> Suddenly a man, in foreign garments: wonderfully real and distinct to look at: stood outside the window, with an ax stuck in his belt, and leading by the bridle an ass laden with wood.
>
> 'Why, it's Ali Baba!' Scrooge exclaimed in ecstasy.[71]

32

It is fiction, not fact, that begins to thaw his mind. These are the images that begin the process of reclaiming Scrooge's lost links with human sympathy.

This is certainly a narrative intended to teach, and it reminds us that Scrooge's first and most valuable lessons, the lessons that made his reanimation possible, were derived from books. But they are story-books, rather than textbooks. The tales that helped the boy Scrooge were those that gave him models for the endurance of loss, loneliness, and betrayal, as Crusoe and Ali Baba do. Yet in *A Christmas Carol* Scrooge is not taught by the printed page; though we, as Dickens's readers, can only experience the lessons of his story in that way. Like the heroes who delighted him in his neglected boyhood, he confronts and defeats his own isolation. In Dickens's hands, the image of Scrooge has joined those of Ali Baba, or Robinson Crusoe, among the cast of fictional characters who embody a national sense of imaginative identity. Reflecting as he does the redemptive power of memory, Scrooge has never been forgotten. He has become one of the channels through which the creative divisions in Victorian thinking about education have been carried deep into our culture.

Dickens believes in the extension of learning, but when it has the nature of programmed schooling he starts to get anxious. Ignorance dehumanizes children, and can make them threatening. But so too can the wrong kind of instruction. Dickens repeatedly warns his readers of the consequences of the sort of education that removes the child from the imaginative resources of feeling, or from the bonds of family affection. The doomed Paul Dombey, the unhappy pupils of M'Choakumchild, or the miserable victims of Dotheboys Hall are aspects of an uneasy pattern in his work, as he returns to the disastrous operations of misguided schooling over and over again. It is not a coincidence that the children Dickens sees as made actively dangerous by inhuman teaching practices are boys. In *Hard Times* (1854), the novel in which Dickens is most openly and polemically preoccupied with educational issues, Sissy Jupe suffers as a consequence of Gradgrind's wrong-headed educational theories. But she finally emerges unscathed, while the ruthless Bitzer does not. Louisa

Gradgrind has her life ruined, but it is Tom Gradgrind who threatens to ruin the lives of others. The pathetic but sinister figure of Ignorance in *A Christmas Carol* is a boy, while the sufferings of Want are represented by a girl. Dickens was not inclined to deny the primacy of masculine intelligence. But for him, as for many of his contemporaries, it was girls, associated as they were with values of emotion and nurture, who could most fully represent the work of a complete education.

In *Our Mutual Friend* (1865), another novel persistently concerned with education, Lizzie Hexam's most significant acts of reading are her interpretations of images in the fire, while her educated brother Charlie can only make destructive use of his newly acquired literacy. Lizzie's reading is prefigured in that of the furnace-keeper in *The Old Curiosity Shop* (1840–1), where the gentle child Nell is told of the kind of literacy that is possible for the neglected poor. Like Lizzie, the furnace-keeper patiently reads the fire:

> 'It's like a book to me,' he said – 'the only book I ever learned to read; and many an old story it tells me. It's music, for I should know its voice among a thousand, and there are other voices in its roar. It has its pictures too. You don't know how many strange faces and different scenes I trace in the red-hot coals. It's my memory, that fire, and shows me all my life.'[72]

Humanized by his elemental reading, the furnace-keeper is among those who help Nell and her grandfather on their hard journey. The fire has taught him to translate his memory of loss, as he recalls his father's death and his loneliness as a child, into compassion: 'when I saw you in the street to-night, you put me in mind of myself, as I was after he died, and made me wish to bring you to the old fire. I thought of those old times again, when I saw you sleeping by it. You should be sleeping now. Lie down again, poor child, lie down again!'[73] The ignorant workman, instructed only by his wordless but warming book, has received the moral education necessary to take on a nurturing role in Nell's friendless life.

When we do – rather rarely – encounter generous teaching in Dickens's fiction, it is likely to come from a girl, and to take place in the setting of domestic warmth. Florence helping her brother Paul with his doleful studies in *Dombey and Son* (1848), or Biddy, a teacher of whom Dickens wholly approves, patiently teaching Pip and Joe to read in *Great Expectations* (1860–1) are representative examples. Here is the kind of education, motivated by compassion rather than duty or ambition, that Dickens favours. This is the loving tuition that the other untaught Jo, Jo the crossing-sweeper in *Bleak House* (1852–3), who functions as a meeker and more engaging version of the scowling Ignorance glimpsed by Scrooge, never receives. Women who teach in schools in any kind of professional capacity often get short shrift in Dickens's fiction. *Dombey and Son*'s Miss Blimber is an image of the unsexing that seemed to Dickens to be imposed on women who teach in an institutional setting:

> There was no light nonsense about Miss Blimber. She kept her hair short and crisp, and wore spectacles. She was dry and sandy with working in the graves of deceased languages. None of your live languages for Miss Blimber. They must be dead – stone dead – and then Miss Blimber dug them up like a Ghoule.[74]

The miniaturized and frustrated Miss Peecher in *Our Mutual Friend* provides a late example of his dismay at new national systems of teacher training as they affected women. Emma Peecher, hopelessly in love with her fellow teacher Bradley Headstone, is

> A little pincushion, a little housewife, a little book, a little workbox, a little set of tables and weights and measures, and a little woman, all in one. She could write a little essay on any subject, exactly a slate long, beginning at the left-hand top of one side and ending at the right-hand bottom of another, and the essay should be strictly according to rule.[75]

Dickens habitually approves of smallness in women – the virtues of Little Dorrit, or Little Nell, are closely associated with their diminutive stature. But here tininess has become a sign of limitation rather than courage. The undersized Miss Peecher is identified as the product of the pupil–teacher apprenticeship system established by James Kay-Shuttleworth in 1846, which allowed for certification of competence in teaching by government examination. Kay-Shuttleworth described his expectations of his newly certificated teachers: 'We hoped to inspire them with a large sympathy for their own class. To implant in their minds the thought that their chief honour would be to aid in rescuing their class from the misery of ignorance and its attendant vices.'[76] These are precisely the objectives that one might have expected Dickens to applaud. But the disciplined teacher training systems instituted by Kay-Shuttleworth have transformed what should have made Miss Peecher a modest and loving Mrs Headstone into a clockwork travesty of a teacher. When she remarks approvingly to her favourite pupil Sally Anne that 'You are forming an excellent habit of arranging your thoughts clearly', the moment is seen as comic.[77] Sally Anne and her teacher have their minds firmly fixed on Headstone at the time, and his obsessive attachment to Lizzie Hexam. Their thoughts, the reader is asked to understand, are anything but clearly arranged.

Headstone, just as frustrated as Miss Peecher and far more destructive, represents some of Dickens's deepest fears on what can happen when the processes of education go seriously wrong. The industrious and highly qualified Headstone might seem to be a legitimate response to the ghost's warning. But his pedagogy is motivated by rigid ambition. Headstone's nature has been poisoned by the mechanical processes that have made him an educator, and the teaching he gives and receives ends in death and disgrace. As an aspiring teacher, he has become the living embodiment of the grim headstone that haunts *A Christmas Carol*. He cannot compete with the lazy but always sexually vital Wrayburn, who emerges victorious in the contest for the love of Lizzie Hexam. The moment when Rogue Riderhood compels the tormented Headstone to write his name on the blackboard is a dark reversal of Scrooge's wiping away his name on his tomb. Riderhood himself reinforces the point:

'I ain't a learned character myself,' said Riderhood, surveying the class, 'but I do admire learning in others. I should dearly like to hear these here young folks read that there name off, from the writing.'

The arms of the class went up. At the miserable master's nod, the shrill chorus arose: 'Bradley Headstone!'

'No?' cried Riderhood. 'You don't mean it? Headstone! Why, that's in a churchyard.'[78]

Headstone's corrosively disciplined identity can only bring about the destruction of his happiness. The fear that unbending systems of education could undermine the kind of modestly contented domesticity that Dickens saw as indispensable to social order made him deeply uncomfortable with the institutionalized movements from which Bradley Headstone and Miss Peecher had emerged. When the educated Headstone looks into the fire, it is cold destruction, not the warmth of charity, which claims him:

Rigid before the fire, as if it were a charmed flame that was turning him old, he sat, with the dark lines deepening in his face, its stare becoming more and more haggard, its surface turning whiter and whiter as if it were being overspread by ashes, and the very texture and colour of his hair degenerating.[79]

Like Arnold's Empedocles, Bradley Headstone is annihilated by his pursuit of knowledge precisely because it is really a desire for something else. But Dickens sees his incineration as a matter of wilful self-destruction, not of tragedy.

In *The Haunted Man*, a supernatural fable published in 1848 as the last of the series of five Christmas books that he had begun with *A Christmas Carol*, Dickens gives explicit voice to his fear that knowledge could exist without feeling, or even replace it. Redlaw, the haunted man of the title, is Dickens's only fictional representation of a university teacher. Gloomy and isolated, he is far from encouraging as an example of the profession. Redlaw is a chemist who has dedicated his life to research. In a reversal of Scrooge's visitation by the ghost of memory, Redlaw is tempted to make a bargain with a malevolent visiting phantom, who offers him the false comfort of oblivion. He will lose nothing of his scientific learning, the ghost promises, but he will forget the people he has known, loved, and lost. Misguidedly renouncing memories of grief and injustice in order to be free of their pain, Redlaw finds that their erasure leaves him scarcely human. Worse still, the phantom has endowed him with the power to obliterate the memories of others. To his dismay, he finds that his presence spreads a spirit of callous discontent wherever he goes. Scrooge is liberated by the supernatural agency of his three visiting phantoms, but in Redlaw's case, the uninvited phantom that troubles his solitude is an evil *doppelgänger*, a projection of his own willed withdrawal and bitterness. No mysteriously otherworldly philanthropy can rescue him from his self-constructed misery. He is led to better things by Milly, an uneducated but maternal woman of the kind that carries Dickens's moral values throughout his fiction. Like Redlaw, Milly's representative status removes her from any kind of realism. She is simply the embodiment of self-effacing domestic affection, as Redlaw is the reflection of its loss. The dismal figure of Redlaw implausibly combines contemporary science in his pioneering chemistry with the image of the traditional scholar in his 'solitary and vault-like' library.[80] We are told that he is 'a teacher on whose lips and hands a crowd of aspiring ears and eyes hung daily', who has made his home in 'an old, retired part of an ancient endowment for students'.[81] Redlaw's status as a forward-looking practising chemist must be taken on trust, for it is his connection with the moribund relics of forgotten learning that Dickens chooses to underline. Like Scrooge, whose association with the modern world of competitive capitalism is improbably coupled with dusty dilapidation in his living quarters, Redlaw lives among the lifeless shadows of the past, 'remote in fashion, age, and custom; so quiet, yet so thundering with echoes when a distant voice was raised or a door was shut, – echoes, not confined to the many low passages and empty rooms, but rumbling and grumbling till they were stifled in the heavy air of the forgotten Crypt where the Norman arches were half-buried in the earth.'[82] These are not the life-giving 'latent' echoes that connect Scrooge with his own past, when he is conducted into the memories of his schoolroom. Instead, Redlaw is surrounded by memories of dead learning. The identification of masculine learning with death and decay, a persistent image in the literature of the period, is here rendered with Gothic intensity. Redlaw must learn to defer to the different authority of Milly's feminine generosity: '... he put his arm though hers, and walked beside her; not as if he were the wise and learned man to whom the wonders of Nature were an open book, and hers were the uninstructed mind, but as if their two positions were reversed, and he knew nothing, and she all.'[83]

Published at the end of a year in which political insurgency briefly seemed an immediate threat to the stability of England, *The Haunted Man* is a particularly forceful example of widely shared misgivings about the limits of education. Unusually insistent, even for Dickens, in its advocation of feminized domesticity as the strongest and safest repository of social value, *The Haunted Man* strenuously rejects the public processes of education as a trustworthy means of resisting social disorder. Without the emotional resources of memory, and without the courage to accept the pain that is inevitably part of its action, Redlaw becomes a destructive force who loosens the bonds that should properly connect all those he encounters. It is not, Dickens tells his readers, the publicly authorized memory of history, but the personal recollection of love and duty and a different sort of knowing, that can avert the danger of revolution. Dickens's troubled thinking about what teaching should be, as he tries to negotiate between competing ideals of communal and domestic models for education, reflects some of the deepest questions that the Victorians were asking themselves about the direction their culture should take.

This is not simply a matter of social conservatism versus liberalism – progressives advocating efficient education for all, conservatives fearing the social consequences of giving too much liberating information to the poor. Its origins are more complex than that, and older too. They extend into the deepest foundations of modern thinking about the functions and limitations of learning. Aristotle, the champion of the disciplines of education, had claimed that poetry was stronger than history in its understanding of moral truth, because its imaginative reach was not constrained by the boundaries of fact. Plato had worried that the authority of memory would be eroded by the priority of written text. For Dickens, it is living memory above all that is the source of moral identity and purpose. Sissy Jupe is safeguarded by the tender memory of her lost father, who might return for his nine oils, just as Lizzie Hexam's loyalty to her father protects her from the misguided ambition that devastates her brother Charlie. It is the painful process of reconnection with his own memories of love and loyalty that can deliver Scrooge from his spiritual death.

Dickens's concerns were endlessly disputed in the middle decades of the nineteenth century. The consequences of these debates for national policy were surprisingly various and, like Dickens's thinking on the matter, often contradictory. They were grounded in the most intense conflicts of the period, to do with religion, the role of the state in national life, social class and social mobility, and changing constructions of gender and sexuality. There was no consensus as to what education was *for* – or who should get it, what should be taught, how it should be taught. On the one hand, it seemed clear that an educated population would be likelier to resist the forces of disruption or violence. The literate and well-informed would be less susceptible to drunkenness and riot, less ready to listen to rabble-rousing demagogues, generally inclined to be more respectable, hard-working and manageable. On the other hand, education might make people ambitious or discontented in ways that could disrupt social stability. Women would no longer be satisfied with marriage and motherhood; indispensable manual workers might want to abandon their ploughs and lathes and hammers. These were obstinate political and cultural problems, of a kind that we have hardly yet succeeded in resolving. As far as scholarly Victorianists have been concerned, they are largely a matter of social history, and many have done invaluable work in tracing the twists and turns on the path to universal free compulsory schooling at the end of the nineteenth century. But we should also attend to the complex resonances of the story as they were perceived among those Victorians who, seeking to heal the divisions, worked towards the spread of serious and well-informed factual training, while also reaching for the liberation of feeling and imagination that would represent a complete education.

Chapter 2

Religious Learning

Changing Balances

The influence of formal schooling expanded throughout the Victorian period. Meanwhile, the certainty of religion, reflecting convictions that had underpinned education for centuries, was in retreat. Scientific discoveries, accompanied by growing sophistication in historical scholarship, undermined trust in the literal truth of biblical teaching. Cultural and political changes challenged the temporal power of churchmen. But this did not mean that matters of faith gently faded from sight. The Victorians were responding to a culture in which familiar balances of power were shifting, and there were movements backwards and forwards. This was also a period of religious revival, as believers were roused into new intensities of self-examination and self-assertion. If these were years in which orthodoxies were defeated, they also saw a surprisingly fervent blossoming of devotion. Historians and literary scholars working on the Victorian period have increasingly turned away from the twentieth-century supposition that the progress towards secularization was a steady and inexorable advance, sweeping all before it.[1] Religion continued to dominate the national consciousness, even among those who were no longer religious. Nowhere are the creative consequences of that new thinking more evident than in Victorian schooling. What was the relation of education to religion? What should it be? And how are those Victorian questions still important to us if, as I have argued, our thinking about education takes the Victorian period as its founding matrix for subsequent developments?

Some Victorians hoped that education would take on the work that had formerly been the business of the churches. The problem with any such aspiration lay in the fact that the functions of religion had been so various, so pervasive and so contradictory. Religious ideologies had provided justifications for class divisions, gender identity, the exercise of political power and control. They championed the status quo, preserving the structures of social status and order. Then as now, the British monarch was both the head of state and the supreme governor of the Church of England. Yet the final authority of the churches had to rest on the claim that they represented unchanging divine truths, not the requirements of political expedience. Revolutionaries could also call on the authority of God in overturning established dispensations of thought, and they often did. The potential for radicalism and conservatism co-exists in the life of religion. Education, for so long the servant of belief, now found itself confronting its ambivalence. Like religion, education would often defend the interests of the powerful social groups which dominated its administration. But it could also undermine their claims to supremacy, for it offered people a richer understanding of human experience, and provided them with practical ways of changing their place in the world. Schooling was sometimes meanly oppressive, but it might bring a generous learning that could transform lives at the deepest level. Often, like religion, education mixed all of these capabilities, evolving complex patterns of influence that made it difficult to sustain a single perspective on its cultural role. What does emerge with clarity from these disputes is that Victorian education was animated by many of the ideals that had previously found their home in religious faith, in ways that often account for the passion with which ideals of learning were pursued. Religion and education may have often found themselves at odds, but they were never wholly separate.

43

They are still connected. The place of religion in school curricula remains profoundly contentious. 'Faith schools' enjoy much favour, among aspiring parents (whether or not their own faith is secure) and with the leading politicians who have repeatedly demonstrated their support for such institutions. But many are suspicious of explicitly religious teaching, and the rising prominence of fundamentalism has sharpened these anxieties. This is one of the most persistent ways in which our ideas have been formed, or obfuscated, by their unrecognized origins in Victorian thinking. If we once thought that religion would inevitably become irrelevant to the national provision of education, recent events have changed our minds. The issues have been with us for a long time, and they are not yet ready to disappear. Behind their specific implications for policy and practice within schools lie still larger and more demanding questions, to do with our shared hopes for the education of our children. If schooling is to be something more than the transmission of quantifiable facts and skills, if we want its formal processes to allow room for the growth of moral and imaginative values, how are we to respond to the decline in the cultural authority of religion? Where are these values to come from? What might the consequences be, if we decide that they cannot be the business of teachers? In this chapter, I want to look at the roots of these dilemmas in nineteenth-century thinking, in an attempt to inform our own understanding of the work of education.

Evangelical Seriousness

In thinking about the longstanding association between belief and learning, we need to be aware that the story is influenced by a variety of social considerations. For the Victorians, the assumption of a recognizably religious identity was not just a matter for private preference. A public allegiance to faith, of whatever kind, was a basic qualification for respectability, and often for employability too. Here it is worth remembering how the religious history of the nineteenth century unfolded. The spread of a serious-minded Evangelicalism was first among the forces that galvanized religion in the early Victorian period. It made the link between social and religious conformity, already strong, still more pervasive. In 1824, the leading Evangelical politician William Wilberforce wrote to his fellow campaigner Hannah More about the central role of religion in schools, and its effect on public morality. He comments on

> the greatly improved state of society in this country since I came into life, and of the hopeful promises of future good, which this moral advancement holds out to us. Everywhere schools; and schools in which religious instruction is attended to – I met fresh traces, my dear friend, of the blessed effects of your writings.[2]

The increasing prevalence of such views meant that religious teaching in schools for both the poor and the affluent became more vigorous. Ensuring the orderly conduct of pupils became a priority in their management. Evangelicals saw self-control as the visible expression of a devout life. It was a belief wholeheartedly shared by nonconformists, who had laid the foundations for this great change in manners. However, their part in cultural and political life in the earlier decades of the nineteenth century was more marginal, which lessened the impact of dissenting expectations of a sober bearing. Evangelicals suffered no such handicaps, for they were not excluded from the universities or the Church of England, and had the support of many fashionable or aristocratic families. They extended their influence deep into the religious and cultural establishment. Degrees of freedom in behaviour that had been permissible in the earlier decades of the century increasingly came to seem coarse, or impious. It is hard to over-estimate the extent of this revolution, whose consequences extend far beyond the lives of convinced Evangelicals. No one could be wholly untouched by it. The tone of earnest gravity that dominated the lives of the Victorians might now seem naive, or pompous, or laughable, but for those who lived through the period it was the atmosphere that all but the most defiant had to breathe. Self-restraint, sexual temperance, hard work and philanthropy – those were the qualities that meant you were taking your life seriously, and that supposition was confirmed by the energies of Evangelicalism and dissent.

This might look like nothing more than the kind of Victorian repression that we are only too glad to have escaped. But at its strongest, an education in religion could serve as a genuinely stimulating foundation for character and conduct. The literature of the period, whether or not it was the product of Evangelical conviction, repeatedly considers the effects of such an education. Elizabeth Missing Sewell, a prolific novelist and also a successful teacher, founded her life's work on her exploration of how religious integrity should express itself in the world. She saw the authority of religion as the only means by which introspection could be prevented from slipping into selfish indulgence. 'Nothing which makes us concentrate our thoughts upon ourselves can be good for any length of time, and self-examination is of all things the most likely to degenerate into morbid self-consciousness, if it was not carried on in a strictly religious spirit.'[3] What makes Sewell's fiction powerful as an expression of a religious understanding of life is her focus on the daily wear-and-tear of human relations. The abstractions of theology do not interest her. She is concerned with what a cultivated religious intelligence might mean for the real education of her characters. The disciplines of religion matter to her because they are the means of learning how to live with scrupulous compassion. In *Katharine Ashton* (1854), Katharine's stubborn father aspires to think on a grander scale, but lacks the insight which religious training has honed in his daughter:

> He was deficient in that quick instinct which gave Katharine a clue to the working of character upon future events. He could see great things, and reason upon them; but he was blind to little things. And yet upon little things the fate, not only of Mr. Ashton's family, but of the whole world must depend: since great things are but the conglomeration of small ones.[4]

Sewell draws on the seventeenth-century Anglican poet George Herbert for her epigraph to *Katharine Ashton*: 'Pitch thy behaviour low; thy projects high.'[5] This is a clue to her own early allegiances, for Herbert was much admired among the Tractarian reformers with whose party Sewell was associated as a young woman. But the sectarian controversies of the period seemed to her largely a distraction from the issues that count. Religious education as she understood it was a training of the spirit alongside the intellect. The value of such training, both in and out of school, was the real point.

The complication here, and the danger too, lay in the uncertain relation between the externally recognizable traits of faith and the moral substance of which they were supposed to be the sign. A religious identity of the kind that Sewell valued worked from within, silently transforming the sources of thought and feeling. More public displays of zeal might simply be false, or self-deceiving. If so, they could hardly be reliable as an indication of social or spiritual distinction, still less as a qualification for teaching. Charles Dickens values the education, moral rather than intellectual, which leads to a sympathetic understanding of the distress of others, together with an active inclination to do something about it. In his novels, paraded godliness invariably hides corruption. He provides an extravagant image of Evangelical sanctimony in the clergyman Chadband, one of many assaults on the failures of charitable education in *Bleak House*. Chadband's hypocritical relations with the poverty-bitten child Jo are exposed by his language, where display takes the place of meaning:

'My young friend,' says Chadband, 'you are to us a pearl, you are to us a diamond, you are to us a gem, you are to us a jewel. And why, my young friend?'

'*I* don't know,' replies Jo. 'I don't know nothink.'

'My young friend,' says Chadband, 'it is because you know nothing that you are to us a gem and jewel. For what are you, my young friend? Are you a beast of the field? No. A bird of the air? No. A fish of the sea or river? No. You are a human boy, my young friend. A human boy. O glorious to be a human boy! And why glorious, my young friend? Because you are capable of receiving the lessons of wisdom, because you are capable of profiting by this discourse which I now deliver for your good, because you are not a stick, or a staff, or a stock, or a stone, or a post, or a pillar.

> O running stream of sparkling joy
> To be a soaring human boy!

And do you cool yourself in that stream now, my young friend? No. Why do you not cool yourself in that stream now? Because you are in a state of darkness, because you are in a state of obscurity, because you are in a state of sinfulness, because you are in a state of bondage. My young friend, what *is* bondage? Let us, in a spirit of love, inquire.'

At this threatening stage of the discourse, Jo, who seems to have been gradually going out of his mind, smears his right arm over his face and gives a terrible yawn. Mrs Snagsby indignantly expresses her belief that he is a limb of the arch-fiend.

'My friends,' says Mr Chadband, with his persecuted chin folding itself into its fat smile again as he looks round, 'it is right that I should be humbled, it is right that I should be tried, it is right that I should be mortified, it is right that I should be corrected. I stumbled, on Sabbath last, when I thought with pride of my three hours' improving. The account is now favourably balanced; my creditor has accepted a composition. O let us be joyful, joyful! O let us be joyful!'[6]

This stream of nonsense is irresistibly comic, but Dickens wants us to understand that Chadband's neglect of his duties towards Jo does real harm. His discourse of love and joy is entirely divorced from the greed that is his unacknowledged motive. When the language of teaching is divided from the hidden priorities of a self-interested speaker, education is poisoned at its roots.

As a religious teacher, Chadband is not only a failure, he is a menace. He is also contemptible. No reader of *Bleak House* has ever wasted any respect on Chadband. Dickens was not alone in identifying the qualities that he condemns in Chadband's 'fat smile' with a failure of the personal authenticity that was the true foundation of human value in religion. In *Rachel Ray* (1863), Anthony Trollope concedes the sincerity of his Evangelical clergyman, Mr Prong. Prong is not a monster of Chadband's stamp. But his demonstrative display of righteousness is coarse because it is no longer real. It has become a charade, the means to an ulterior end. Trollope, unlike Dickens, saw this as a failure of gentility. He is

> deficient in one vital qualification for a clergyman of the Church of England; he was not a gentleman ... I do not mean to say that he was a thief or a liar; nor do I mean to complain that he picked his teeth with a fork and misplaced his 'h's. I am by no means prepared to define what I do mean, – thinking, however, that most men and most women will understand me.[7]

The fact that he is called 'Prong' says much, for it is not a dignified name. Like Dickens, Trollope will sometimes direct his readers in the naming of his characters. The name of Obadiah Slope, the obnoxious Evangelical chaplain in *Barchester Towers*, is also a clear pointer. No gentleman could carry such a name in a novel by Trollope – sloppy (Trollope hints that he is descended from Laurence Sterne's Dr Slop), and not on the level. Like Chadband, Slope is oily and repulsive:

> His hair is lank and of a dull pale reddish hue. It is always formed into three straight lumpy masses, each brushed with admirable precision, and cemented with much grease; two of them adhere closely to the sides of his face, and the other lies at right angles above them. He wears no whiskers and is always punctiliously shaven. His face is nearly of the same colour as his hair, though perhaps a little redder: it is not unlike beef – beef, however, one would say, of a bad quality. His forehead is capacious and high, but square and heavy, and unpleasantly shining. His mouth is large, though his lips are thin and bloodless, and his big, prominent, pale-brown eyes inspire anything but confidence. His nose, however, is his redeeming feature: it is pronounced, straight, and well-formed; though I myself should have liked it better

did it not possess a somewhat spongy, porous appearance, as though it had been cleverly formed out of a red-coloured cork.[8]

Slope's greasy shine combines a sense of uncleanness with carnality. But physical self-indulgence is not what is most repellent in Slope. What is more insidious, and more menacing, is his hunger for power. Scheming to achieve his ends through the cold perversion of the inwardness that characterizes Evangelical fervour, Slope practises a callous politics of the soul. He is a predator:

> He cares nothing, one way or the other, for the Queen's supremacy; these to his ears are empty words, meaning nothing. Forms he regards but little, and such titular expressions as supremacy, consecration, ordination, and the like convey of themselves no significance to him. Let him be supreme who can. The temporal king, judge, or gaoler can work but on the body. The spiritual master, if he have the necessary gifts and can duly use them, has a wider field of empire. He works upon the soul. If he can make himself be believed, he can be all powerful over those who listen. If he be careful to meddle with none who are too strong in intellect, or too weak in flesh, he may indeed be supreme. And such was the ambition of Mr Slope.[9]

This was hardly the ambition that enterprising middle-class parents who might be reading Dickens or Trollope would wish to see in their children. A recognizably religious identity might be necessary for respectability, and it could offer the possibility of a genuine moral vitality. But if the religion were not the real thing, spiritual and social aspirations would be shipwrecked together. Chadband, Prong and Slope cannot claim the honour that is due to Christian gentlemen, because their purposes are confined to the gratification of self-interested impulses they have been able neither to understand nor to control. Their limitations condemn them to inferiority. In the eyes of both this world and the next, they are second-rate. 'When people are thoroughly Christian, they become also thoroughly well-bred', as one of Sewell's more optimistic characters remarked.[10] Here Sewell means breeding in the sense of education, rather than birth. Seen in these terms, the stakes are high. If hollow mediocrity is to be avoided, an authentic religious education – something more than the dissemination of a show of belief, concealing opportunism – would be called for.

Educating Clergymen

One of the cultural factors that intervened in the relation between religion and education in the Victorian period was the position of the Anglican church, an institution which was losing its political power but still carried a good deal of social prestige. Its identity was supported by the schools and colleges that affirmed its doctrines and trained its clergymen. A degree from Oxford and Cambridge, the only English universities until the first alternatives began to emerge in the nineteenth century, qualified men for ordination into the Church of England. In the sleepier periods of the universities' history, the teaching on offer was far from incendiary. The cleric and wit Sydney Smith was a fellow of Oxford's New College in the late eighteenth century, and later wrote scathingly about the experience: 'A genuine Oxford tutor would shudder to hear his young men disputing upon moral and political truth, forming and pulling down theories, and indulging in all the boldness of youthful discussion. He would augur nothing from it, but impiety to God, and treason to kings.'[11] The association between university and church lingered throughout the nineteenth century, and beyond. Entry to both institutions continued to be primarily governed by social class rather than intellectual ambition, or religious vocation. Those who approved of this pattern sometimes did so because they had never given the matter a moment's thought. Others, like Trollope, felt that the identity of a gentleman meant more than privilege and wealth. It was a question of character and understanding. In addressing the Oxford Diocesan Society in 1866, Bishop Samuel Wilberforce, the son of William Wilberforce, boasted that the ministry of the Church of England has been *hitherto* and is *at this time*, filled by gentlemen of the nation of England, by men who have had a gentle education, and who have come – yea, and in most numerous cases of gentle, and even of the highest blood of this land and who have entered the Church with all that distinctive formation of character which comes of such an education and such an inheritance.[12]

Samuel Wilberforce's resonantly rhetorical 'yea' here is a revealing gesture, implying as it does that the social and educational distinction of English clergymen has the dignity of biblical sanction.

The widely shared assumption that only a gentleman could properly serve as a clergyman in the Church of England meant that ordination as a clergyman was seen as in itself a mark of gentility. Here too, social and spiritual ambitions inevitably became entangled. As a young man, the art critic John Ruskin, whose family controlled a charitable nomination to the highly-esteemed schooling offered by Christ's Hospital in London, wrote to a college friend about the pleas for support they received. An ardent Evangelical at this point in his life, Ruskin derides those who see education simply as the means to the social status and secure income that a successful career in the church might bring:

> Letters from widowed mothers, who always say that they 'haven't means to bring up their children in the *station* of *life* they have been accustomed to'. The mothers are always willing to work, one sees that; they don't find their children a bore. It is their confounded vanity that upsets them; they can make their shirts and their shifts, but they can't make 'em surplices; and as mothers always want their eldest sons to have a university education, and be bishops – and their second son to be Lord Chancellor – and their third, admiral of the blue – they try Christ's Hospital as the first step.[13]

The visions of social glory that Ruskin mocks are crowned with success in the church. It is the episcopal mitre that the widowed mothers dream of as the pinnacle of glory for their eldest sons; becoming Lord Chancellor, or an admiral, cannot quite compare.

Years later, Ruskin sardonically recalled that his own father had entertained similar fantasies:

> His ideal of my future, – now entirely formed in conviction of my genius, – was that I should enter at college into the best society, take all the prizes every year, and a double first to finish with; marry Lady Clara Vere de Vere, write poetry as good as Byron's, only pious; preach sermons as good as Bossuet's, only Protestant; be made, at forty, Bishop of Winchester, and at fifty, Primate of England.[14]

For Ruskin, a serious responsibility to a spiritual vocation meant quite a different kind of education, put to a wholly different use. In his view, religion must always come first. There could be no argument on the matter.

> Now you all know, that anything which makes religion its second object, makes religion *no* object. God will put up with a great many things in the human heart, but there is one thing He will *not* put up with in it – a second place. He who offers God a second place, offers Him no place. And there is another mighty truth which you all know, that he who makes religion his first object, makes it his whole object; he has no other work in the world than God's work.[15]

The social advantages of piety were a trivial matter, seen in those uncompromising terms. But parents were ambitious for their children, as Ruskin's proud father had been hopeful for his boy. It remained clear that for some young men ordination brought solid rewards in this world. Patrick Brontë, father of Charlotte, Emily and Anne, escaped prospects of a life of drudgery on a farm in County Down by gaining admittance to St John's College Cambridge in 1802. Succeeding where Thomas Hardy's fictional Jude was to fail, he achieved a degree that enabled him to become an Anglican minister, and finally incumbent of Haworth Parsonage – an exceptional ascent for a young man without the help of family money or social connections. This was a route closed to women, but they took a close interest in the gentlemen who pursued it. Observers often commented with some asperity on the sexual success of clergymen among the young ladies of the parish. Charlotte Brontë was inclined to a cynical view of the 'abundant shower of curates'[16] whose falling on the land she identified as one of the defining features of the age she lived in; but when she married, it was Arthur Bell Nicholls, her father's curate, that she chose as her husband. The resolute governess heroine of Anne Brontë's novel *Agnes Grey* (1847) accepts the marriage proposal of Mr Weston, a high-minded curate. Her choice is seen as the proper fulfilment of her emotional, sexual and spiritual needs, but it is also an affirmation of her standing as a gentlewoman. One of the reasons that religion continued to matter as an element of education was that it could confirm and perhaps promote the gentility of a child. Parents knew this very well, and looked to schools to provide the teaching, and the example, that would enable their children to claim the social and economic benefits that might accompany a middle-class identity.

As the century progressed, and the intellectual confidence of religion ebbed, ambitious young men found it harder to reconcile ecclesiastical ambition with a rigorous education. Ninety years after Patrick Brontë's matriculation at Cambridge, the novelist George Gissing describes Mrs Peak, mother of the poor but talented Godwin, still looking to the church to provide a way forward for her son: 'Godwin, how would you like to go to College and be a clergyman?' The scientifically-inclined Godwin resists – 'I don't want to be a parson.'[17] But later he chooses to feign religious belief, and even plans to enter the Anglican ministry, in order to win the affection of the refined young lady he loves, and qualify himself to join her social circle. Peak's calculated pretence is exposed, and he dies in lonely misery. In 1895, Thomas Hardy could still touch this raw nerve in his condemnation of the closed complacencies of Christminster, his fictional version of Oxford. In *Jude the Obscure*, a humble stonemason like Jude will find no entry to Biblioll College, no matter how diligently he toils over his books. The master of the college responds to Jude's hopeful enquiry in perfectly straightforward terms:

I have read your letter with interest; and, judging from your description of yourself as a working-man, I venture to think that you will have a much better chance of success in life by remaining in your own sphere and sticking to your trade than by adopting any other course. That, therefore, is what I advise you to do.[18]

Class still counts for more than the classics as a qualification for entry. But Hardy is also wryly critical of the mingled idealism and worldly ambition that had motivated Jude's wish to enter Christminster:

And then he continued to dream, and thought he might become even a bishop by leading a pure, energetic, wise, Christian life. And what an example he would set! If his income were £5000 a year, he would give away £4500 in one form and another, and live sumptuously (for him) on the remainder. Well, on second thoughts, a bishop was absurd. He would draw the line at an archdeacon. Perhaps a man could be as good and as learned and as useful in the capacity of archdeacon as in that of bishop. Yet he thought of the bishop again.[19]

The pathos of Jude's ill-directed hopes lies in the fact that he has not fully understood his own purposes, nor the futility of the goals that have caught his imagination. In the mid-1890s his plight is beginning to look old-fashioned. Broader choices were beginning to open up for boys in his situation. The jumbled aspirations that destroy Jude are a product of lingering confusions within Victorian religion, learning, ambition, conformity and class. These perplexities were slow to dissolve.

The potential for a productive relation between religion and education was diluted by other considerations. But this association was not inevitably encumbered by the social ambitions that Trollope and Dickens had condemned. Religion's capacity to think beyond economic necessity could open the way to personal models for learning. Energy of this kind, still essential for our own lives, need not be imprisoned within theological codes or repressive ecclesiastical traditions. The question for us is how we might free the potential richness of such an education from the cultural constraints that have diminished its potential in the past.

A Complete Education

Religious devotion was usually expressed within a denominational context, and for many this was still part of the point. Anglican schools would produce firm young Anglicans; Nonconformist schools would guarantee a new generation of committed dissenters. These divisions were also embroiled with distinctions between social classes. The feeling that dissenters were less gentlemanly than Anglicans of any description remained, though it was diluted by the energy and success of many Nonconformist chapels and the families who supported them. But others were convinced that the authenticity of the spiritual impulse mattered more than the particular denominational form that it might take. Dr Thomas Arnold, father of Matthew Arnold, is now chiefly remembered as the reforming headmaster of Rugby School, an institution he took on as a slack and declining minor public school in 1828, and transformed into one of the most influential educational institutions in the country. A firmly committed Anglican, Thomas Arnold nevertheless believed that a commitment to Christianity should outweigh any sectarian affiliation:

> I groan over the divisions of the Church, of all our evils I think the greatest, – of Christ's Church I mean, – that men should call themselves Roman Catholics, Church of England men, Baptists, Quakers, all sorts of various appellations, forgetting that only glorious name of CHRISTIAN, which is common to all, and a true bond of union.[20]

Arnold's aim was to make Christian gentlemen of his pupils. This need not, he believed, be primarily a social ambition, nor one confined to the hierarchies of the Anglican church. The refinement of understanding that would distinguish a true gentleman was the product of spiritual training, impossible without Christian conviction. The cultivation of mental prowess was never the main point for Thomas Arnold, whose order of priorities was clear: 'What we must look for here is, firstly, religious and moral principles; secondly, gentlemanly conduct; thirdly, intellectual ability.'[21] Arnold meant more than good manners by 'gentlemanly conduct', just as Sewell meant more than high birth when she described someone as 'well-bred'. Social distinctions were also moral distinctions for these serious educators, primarily to do with a sensitivity to the feelings and sensibilities of others, and a respect for their needs. For them, gentility was an expression of the maturity of faith, not simply a marker for the hierarchies of class.

Years of hard experience as a headmaster made Thomas Arnold realistic about what was to be expected from the process of a religious education. His pupils arrived as harmless infants, and seemed immediately to be degraded into barbarians by the rough-and-tumble of school life. But it was not his aim to preserve the innocence of those he taught. The experience of wrong is a precondition for an understanding of what is right. Thomas Arnold's account of a boy's growth makes a pilgrimage of education, a painful but necessary preparation for life's trials:

> Believe me, that such questions must and ought to present themselves to the mind of every thinking man who is concerned in the management of a school: and I do think that we could not answer them satisfactorily, that our work would absolutely be unendurable, if we did not bear in mind that our eyes should look forward, and not backward; if we did not remember that the victory of fallen man is to be sought for, not in innocence, but in tried virtue. Comparing only the state of a boy after his first half-year, or year, at school, with his earlier state as a child, and our reflections on the evil of our system would be bitter indeed; but when we compare a boy's state after his first half-year, or year, at school, with what it is afterwards; when we see the clouds again clearing off; when we find coarseness succeeded again by delicacy; hardness and selfishness again broken up, and giving place to affection and benevolence; murmuring and self-will exchanged for humility and self-denial; and the profane, or impure, or false tongue, uttering again only the words of truth and purity; and when we see that all these good things are now, by God's grace, rooted in the character; that they have been tried, and grown up

amidst the trial; that the knowledge of evil has made them hate it the more, and be the more aware of it; then we can look upon our calling with patience, and even with thankfulness; we see that the wilderness has been gone through triumphantly, and that its dangers have hardened and strengthened the traveller for all his remaining pilgrimage.[22]

Arnold's comments highlight the part that gendered values had to play in the construction of gentility. His spiritual ambitions for his pupils remain predominantly masculine, founded on ideals of combative strength. Yet his references to delicacy, affection, purity and self-denial as the desirable products of this training are a reminder that the training of a Christian gentleman was not, as far as he was concerned, simply to be a matter of competitive ruthlessness. His conception of a religious education for boys – and for Thomas Arnold, no other kind was possible – combines the virtues of masculine fortitude with those of feminine delicacy. Charles Dickens feared the dominance of a male brutalism as it might be codified in education, and advocated the domestic teaching of loving wives and mothers as the safeguard against its triumph. For Arnold, only religion could represent the redemptive balance between the values of masculinity and femininity. But this could not be a matter of preserving the innocence of a sexless infancy. Children must be allowed to experience the roughness of life at first hand, and struggle with its challenges, before they can grow as they should. To protect them from this turbulence is to rob them of an essential freedom. Arnold's insistence on the need for this courage should matter to us, given our anxious inclination to safeguard children from all possible harm.

The role of gender in these issues was crucial for the Victorians, and it had major consequences for educational thought and policy. Within British culture, formal learning and its associated purposes had been primarily identified with the interests of boys. Young men were seen as qualified by nature to benefit from the demands of its prestigious public institutions, and from the opportunities they would provide for social advancement. Women might also profit, but their gains would be largely indirect, to be experienced as the daughters, wives and mothers of successful men. Female education would be in a domestic context – either within the home, or in small private schools formed on a family model. This was a pattern that can be seen to persist throughout most of the Victorian period, until legislative and institutional reforms gradually began to introduce wider opportunities for women in the final decades of the nineteenth century.[23] Years before that happened, however, the oppositions of gender, and the hierarchical values assigned to them, came to seem less fixed. If competition and regulation were to govern the reform of education, would the outcome be a meaner and more destructive world? Writers might address the question in terms of imagination, fact and history,[24] but the categories of gender also weighed heavily in the debate. Perhaps the refinement of feeling that Thomas Arnold believed to characterize a gentleman, but which were more commonly identified as the qualities of a lady, might be incorporated into education through the practice of religion. Arnold thought that they could, and folded the divisions of gender into his ideal of an inclusive and unified religion. He did so within the inevitable constraints of a Victorian public school, an institution grounded in repressions of class that we would hardly want to revive. But his passion for a spiritual, moral and intellectual education that allows for the unfolding of the whole child commands respect, and gives his example lasting power.

One reason for the persistence of Arnold's Rugby as a model for schools is the lasting popularity of Thomas Hughes's *Tom Brown's Schooldays* (1857), in which an idealized memory of Hughes's experiences of Rugby under Arnold's leadership is combined with a robustly political interpretation of the implications of education for the national character. Hughes, a Christian socialist and committed supporter of working men's education, cared little for the virtues of scholarship. When the blunt Squire Brown, Tom's father, considers what advice to give as his boy is about to leave for his first term at school, he echoes many of Thomas Arnold's priorities. In the Squire's mind, moral and religious attributes count for more than the classical attainments that were the main business of the school's syllabus, and Tom must acquire those qualities for himself. But Squire Brown, unlike Thomas Arnold, is inclined to entrust women with the first and most formative role in the religious training which is the foundation of his son's education. Seen as an unequivocally manly character, Squire Brown credits the grounding of Tom's faith to the influence and instruction of his mother:

'I won't tell him to read his Bible, and love and serve God; if he don't do that for his mother's sake and teaching, he won't for mine. Shall I go into the sort of temptations he'll meet with? No, I can't do that. Never do for an old fellow to go into such things with a boy. He won't understand me. Do him more harm than good, ten to one. Shall I tell him to mind his work, and say he's sent to school to make himself a good scholar? Well, but he isn't sent to school for that – at any rate, not for that mainly. I don't care a straw for Greek particles, or the digamma; no more does his mother. What is he sent to school for? Well, partly because he wanted so to go. If he'll only turn out a brave, helpful, truth-telling Englishman, and a gentleman, and a Christian, that's all I want,' thought the Squire; and upon this view of the case he framed his last words of advice to Tom, which were well enough suited to his purpose.[25]

Tom's experiences at school confirm this pattern. The Doctor (explicitly modelled on Thomas Arnold), noting a danger of coarseness in Tom's sturdy character, gives him special responsibility for the care of a girlish new pupil, Arthur: 'a slight, pale boy, with large blue eyes and light fair hair, who seemed ready to shrink through the floor.'[26] Tom helps Arthur through the trials of his first months at school, but he learns as much from the newcomer's gentle piety as Arthur gains from Tom's protection. What emerges, in fact, is something approaching a tentative picture of a Christian marriage. The all-male community of a public school functions in Hughes's mind as in part an image of England. Under these fictional circumstances, his representation of mutual help in the friendship between Tom and Arthur is as close as he can get to the notion that a complete education, like a complete religion, must be grounded in the complementary virtues of masculinity and femininity.

The devout and courageous Arthur is a key figure in Tom Brown's English education. Arthur expresses the values of the reformed and principled clerical class that Evangelicalism at its most sincere had created. His father had been a heroic minister, sacrificing his life for his faith and his people, and Arthur inherits his mettle. Arthur's father is the perfect Christian gentleman – he is everything that Trollope's Slope and Dickens's Chadband failed to be. But he is also as stalwart in manliness as Tom's father, the bluff Squire Brown. Hughes is keen to emphasize that his spiritual vocation has not contaminated him with any hint of feminine weakness:

Arthur's father had been the clergyman of a parish in the Midland counties, which had risen into a large town during the war, and upon which the hard years which followed had fallen with fearful weight ... Into such a parish and state of society Arthur's father had been thrown at the age of twenty-five – a young married parson, full of faith, hope, and love. He had battled with it like a man, and had lots of fine Utopian ideas about the perfectibility of mankind, glorious humanity, and such-like, knocked out of his head, and a real, whole-some Christian love for the poor, struggling, sinning men, of whom he felt himself one, and with and for whom he spent fortune, and strength, and life, driven into his heart. He had battled like a man, and gotten a man's reward – no silver tea-pots or salvers, with flowery inscriptions setting forth his virtues and the appreciation of a genteel parish; no fat living or stall, for which he never looked, and didn't care; no sighs and praises of comfortable dowagers and well-got-up young women, who worked him slippers, sugared his tea, and adored him as 'a devoted man'; but a manly respect, wrung from the unwilling souls of men who fancied his order their natural enemies ...
Arthur and his wife both caught the fever, of which he died in a few days ... I must show you what sort of a man it was who had begotten and trained little Arthur, or else you won't believe in him, which I am resolved you shall do; and you won't see how he, the timid, weak boy, had points in him from which the bravest and

61

strongest recoiled, and made his presence and example felt from the first on all sides, unconsciously to himself, and without the least attempt at proselytizing. The spirit of his father was in him, and the Friend to whom his father had left him did not neglect the trust.[27]

'Poor little Arthur', as Hughes is prone to call him, is seen as the embodiment of the generous Christianity that Thomas Arnold had hoped to instil in his pupils. As such, he must carry the values of both femininity and refined masculinity to the young Tom, who is rather too rudely male for his own good.

Tom Brown's Schooldays is not only a book about teaching; it is designed to teach, and also to preach. Hughes, like Trollope, does not shrink from the sermon as his model:

> Several persons, for whose judgement I have the highest respect, while saying very kind things about this book, have added, that the great fault of it is 'too much preaching'; but they hope I shall amend in this matter should I ever write again. Now this I most distinctly decline to do. Why, my whole object in writing at all was to get the chance of preaching! When a man comes to my time of life and has his bread to make, and very little time to spare, is it likely that he will spend almost the whole of his yearly vacation in writing a story just to amuse people? I think not. At any rate, I wouldn't do so myself.[28]

For all his enthusiasm for preaching, Hughes was not inclined to become an ordained clergyman. Like many who urged a religious interpretation of education, he distanced himself from the constraints of sectarian allegiances. His wayward brand of Protestantism led him to produce his own version of the sermon, in which narratives of schooling take the place of formal allegiance to any sanctioned orthodoxy. Instead of serving as a minister, he became an active educationalist and a founding member of the Christian Socialist movement, in which politics often took precedence over theology. Like Ruskin, Hughes was a firm supporter of the Working Men's College established by the Christian Socialists in 1854, and acted as its principal from 1872 to 1883. What emerges in *Tom Brown's*

Schooldays is a fictionalized reflection of Thomas Arnold's concept of education as a pilgrimage, rough and demanding, but with refinement alongside grace as its final purpose.

Hughes has little to say about what Tom Brown gained from his books. Yet he does emphasize Tom's eventual renunciation of the use of 'cribs' to help translate difficult classical texts, prompted by Arthur ('Because you're the honestest boy in Rugby, and that ain't honest'), as a turning point in his journey to maturity.[29] Tom will never be a classical scholar, but the Latin and Greek that he must acquire, as the mark of a gentleman, should be properly his own. Its final purpose is moral, rather than intellectual.

Though many were sympathetic to Hughes's views, not every writer was ready to dismiss the value of a serious intellectual training within religious education. John Henry Newman is a powerful example of a public intellectual who thought that faith and learning were inseparable. The leading figure in Oxford's Tractarian movement, Newman converted to Roman Catholicism in 1845. He was active in the foundation of a new Catholic university in Ireland, and in 1852 he delivered five lectures in a series of *Discourses on the Scope and Nature of University Education*. These later formed the basis of his influential *Idea of a University* (1873). It was Newman's priority to advocate the Catholic faith that he regarded as true for all time. But this need not compromise the practice of a truly liberal education – in fact theological schooling would be an essential part of that learning. A liberal education could be nothing less than the training of the whole mind, resulting in 'the force, the steadiness, the comprehensiveness and the versatility of intellect, the command over our own powers, the instinctive just estimate of things as they pass before us, which sometimes indeed is a natural gift, but commonly is not gained without much effort and the exercise of years.'[30]

Like Thomas Arnold, Newman based these principles on practical experience, for he had worked for many years as a university tutor. This meant that he did not expect the progress of his pupils to be untroubled. Again like Arnold, he sees the qualities of gentility as an indispensable element of what is to be gained from a religious education. But his definition of a gentleman is more than a matter of polite manners. It is part of what he describes as

> real cultivation of mind; and I do not deny that the characteristic excellences of a gentleman are included in it. ... Certainly a liberal education does manifest itself in a courtesy, propriety, and polish of word and action, which is beautiful in itself, and acceptable to others; but it does much more. It brings the mind into form – for the mind is like the body. Boys outgrow their shape and their strength; their limbs have to be knit together, and their constitution needs tone. Mistaking animal spirits for vigour, and over-confident in their health, ignorant what they can bear and how to manage themselves, they are immoderate and extravagant; and fall into sharp sicknesses. This is an emblem of their minds; at first they have no principles laid down within them as a foundation for the intellect to build upon; they have no discriminating convictions, and no grasp of consequences. And therefore they talk at random, if they talk much, and cannot help being flippant, or what is emphatically called '*young*'. They are merely dazzled by phenomena, instead of perceiving things as they are.
>
> It were well if none remained boys all their lives; but what is more common than the sight of grown men, talking on political or moral or religious subjects, in that offhand, idle way, which we signify by the word *unreal*? 'That they simply do not know what they are talking about' is the spontaneous silent remark of any man of sense who hears them. Hence such persons have no difficulty in contradicting themselves in successive sentences, without being conscious of it. Hence others, whose defect in intellectual training is more latent, have their most unfortunate crotchets, as they are called, or hobbies, which deprive them of the influence which their estimable qualities would otherwise secure. Hence others can never look straight before them, never see the point, and have no difficulties in the most difficult subjects. Others are hopelessly obstinate and prejudiced, and, after they have been driven from their opinions, return to them the next moment without even an attempt to explain why. Others are so intemperate and intractable that there is no greater calamity for a good cause than that they should get hold of it.[31]

64

Thomas Arnold, Thomas Hughes and John Henry Newman speak from very different Christian perspectives, but they all promote a religious education that will enable a child to subjugate the arbitrary demands of the self. Each argues that an educated mind is not simply a filing cabinet, efficiently stocked with information. It is a dynamic entity, which must include the possibility for the error and false starts that are inevitable as a child learns. Its lessons might be externally imposed, but if they are not internally possessed, they will be useless, and may even be dangerous. Education that is 'real', to borrow Newman's term, will have both spiritual and practical advantages, nurturing 'a faculty of entering with comparative ease into any subject of thought, and of taking up with aptitude any science or profession.'[32] This is not a vocational training, but it will lead to an adaptable professional competence.

Newman does not slight the acquisition of knowledge as a necessary objective of education. His definition of its benefits is not, however, altogether what we might expect. As he sees it, knowledge is not a collection of facts, or a body of information to be patiently absorbed. It is an active principle, only worthwhile when it is fully assimilated into the life of the mind which possesses it:

> When I speak of Knowledge, I mean something intellectual, something which grasps what it perceives through the senses; something which takes a view of things; which sees more than the senses convey; which reasons upon what it sees, and while it sees; which invests it with an idea. It expresses itself, not in a mere enunciation, but by an enthymeme:[33] it is of the nature of science from the first, and in this consists its dignity. The principle of real dignity in Knowledge, its worth, its desirableness, considered irrespectively of its results, is this germ within it of a scientific or a philosophical process. This is how it comes to be an end in itself; this is why it admits of being called Liberal. Not to know the relative disposition of things is the state of slaves or children; to have mapped out the Universe is the boast, or at least the ambition, of Philosophy.
>
> Moreover, such knowledge is not a mere extrinsic or accidental advantage, which is ours today and another's tomorrow, which may

be got up from a book, and easily forgotten again, which we can command or communicate at our pleasure, which we can borrow for the occasion, carry about in our hand, and take into the market; it is an acquired illumination, it is a habit, a personal possession, and an inward endowment. And this is the reason, why it is more correct, as well as more usual, to speak of a University as a place of education, than of instruction, though, when knowledge is concerned, instruction would at first sight have seemed the more appropriate word. We are instructed, for instance, in manual exercises, in the fine and useful arts, in trades, and in ways of business; for these are methods, which have little or no effect upon the mind itself, are contained in rules committed to memory, to tradition, or to use, and bear upon an end external to themselves. But education is a higher word; it implies an action upon our mental nature, and the formation of a character; it is something individual and permanent, and is commonly spoken of in connexion with religion and virtue. When, then, we speak of the communication of Knowledge as being Education, we thereby really imply that that Knowledge is a state or condition of mind; and since cultivation of mind is surely worth seeking for its own sake, we are thus brought once more to the conclusion, which the word 'Liberal' and the word 'Philosophy' have already suggested, that there is a Knowledge, which is desirable, though nothing come of it, as being of itself a treasure, and a sufficient remuneration of years of labour.[34]

Newman believed that a university must be rooted in Catholic teaching. Its foundations would then be invulnerable, for they would be an expression of certain truth. But this did not mean that its thinking would be immovable. His view of education is a spiritual interpretation of what George Eliot called 'the Development Theory', culminating in scientific terms in the Darwinian concept of evolution as the principle governing all life.[35] An idea is an unstoppable force, like a changing species, which may 'rather be said to use the minds of Christians, than to be used by them'.[36] It grows as it passes through the consciousness that it influences. 'Wonderful it is to see with what effort, hesitation, suspense, interruption – with how many swayings to the right and to the left – with how many reverses, yet with what certainty of advance ... it has been evolved.'[37] The concept of humility lies at the heart of this argument. An energetically evolving idea does not support the ambition of the intelligence that it adopts. The reverse is true. The receiving mind, if it is adequate to the task, will serve the idea, and will fulfil its individual potential in doing so:

> When an idea, whether real or not, is of a nature to arrest and possess the mind, it may be said to have life, that is, to live in the mind which is its recipient. Thus mathematical ideas, real as they are, can hardly properly be called living, at least ordinarily. But, when some great enunciation, whether true or false, about human nature, or present good, or government, or duty, or religion, is carried forward into the public throng of men and draws attention, then it is not merely received passively in this or that form into many minds, but it becomes an active principle within them, leading them to an ever-new contemplation of itself, to an application of it in various directions, and a propagation of it on every side.[38]

Seen in this light, formal or informal education is a matter of building connections, enabling the mind to see beyond self-concern. This is what, in Newman's model, the integration of religion and education means.

The concept of knowledge as a state of mind to be valued for its own sake rather than for its immediate utility was attractive to many of those who were involved in the expansion of the universities in the second half of the nineteenth century, and beyond. Not all saw it in religious terms. Newman's concept of a 'liberal education' could readily be translated into a secular framework. For many years it was a central tenet in the planning of university programmes, though its implications need not be confined to higher education. It is a familiar ideal, now generally dismissed as outdated, perhaps because it became so closely identified with the notion of a gentlemanly learning. Nevertheless, it includes elements that are worth returning to, and I shall do so in my final chapter.

The Uses of Ignorance: John Ruskin

This understanding of education as a process of making connections was shared by many of those who wrote on the subject with the deepest commitment. These authors were influenced by many varieties of Christian belief, and some of the most vigorous were not Christian at all. John Ruskin, like Thomas Hughes, did not become a clergyman, whatever his parents might have hoped. In his middle years he lost his Christian faith. Nevertheless, he devoted his life to a secular interpretation of religious vocation. His writing and his practical work as a teacher were inseparable responsibilities. Ruskin worked alongside Hughes and his colleagues as a tutor in the Working Men's College, where he regularly taught art in the early years of the new institution. Later, he became Oxford's first Professor of Fine Art, and founded his own School of Drawing in the university. Teaching was more than a matter of abstract theory for Ruskin. He knew about its day-to-day demands and pressures. He did not, however, have experience of the kind of institutional education that Hughes describes in *Tom Brown's Schooldays*. He was largely home-educated, by his mother and a series of personal tutors. This gave him a much wider experience of art and natural science than was available to most of his peers, a breadth of learning that he put to positive use in his mature work. Later, Ruskin came to value the education that the right institutions could provide. But what mattered most to him as a child and later as a student at Christ Church Oxford was the learning that he pursued alone, and his early concepts of education are more solitary than most.

In the course of these isolated studies, Ruskin created an individual voice that combined the energies of his mother's Evangelical faith with those of his father's Romantic interests. Both Evangelical Protestantism and Romanticism assumed the primacy of inwardness, a self-forged authenticity that was the only genuine means to mental and spiritual growth. It followed that the passive acceptance of knowledge from human authority, even or perhaps especially the most august institutions, like the Royal Academy or Christ Church, was not the way to a serious education. Ruskin's intensely Protestant understanding of religion and learning meant that he had none of Newman's veneration for the sanctioned supremacy of any church's teaching. True authority comes from God, or from nature as the creation of God, and it must be recreated in the perception and in the feelings of the faithful student. When Ruskin made his entrance on the literary scene in 1843 with the first volume of his monumental defence of the painter J. M. W. Turner, he was 24 years old, and unknown. What made the book revolutionary was his insistence that his readers should test Turner's powers as a landscape painter against their own observations of nature. He amplifies his meaning with accounts of his own experiences. At one point, defending Turner against the charge that his colour is unnaturally exaggerated, Ruskin describes an Italian journey:

It had been wild weather when I left Rome, and all across the Campagna the clouds were sweeping in sulphurous blue, with a clap of thunder or two, and breaking gleams of sun along the Claudian aqueduct lighting up the infinity of its arches like the bridge of chaos. But as I climbed the long slope of the Alban Mount, the storm swept finally to the north, and the noble outline of the domes of Albano, and graceful darkness of its ilex grove, rose against pure streaks of alternate blue and amber; the upper sky gradually flushing through the last fragments of rain-cloud in deep palpitating azure, half æther and half dew. The noonday sun came slanting down the rocky slopes of La Riccia, and their masses of entangled and tall foliage, whose autumnal tints were mixed with the wet verdure of a thousand evergreens, were penetrated with it as with rain. I cannot call it colour, it was conflagration. Purple, and crimson, and scarlet, like the curtains of God's tabernacle, the rejoicing trees sank into the valley in showers of light, every separate leaf quivering with buoyant and burning life; each, as it turned to reflect or to transmit the sunbeam, first a torch and then an emerald. Far up into the recesses of the valley, the green vistas arched like the hollows of mighty waves of some crystalline sea, with the arbutus flowers dashed along their flanks for foam, and silver flakes of orange spray tossed into the air around them, breaking over the grey walls of rock into a thousand separate stars, fading and kindling alternately as the weak wind lifted and let them fall. Every glade of grass burned like the golden floor of heaven, opening in sudden gleams as the foliage broke and closed above it, as sheet-lightning opens in a cloud at sunset; the motionless masses of dark rock – dark though flushed with scarlet lichen, casting their quiet shadows across its restless radiance, the fountain underneath them filling its marble hollow with blue mist and fitful sound; and over all, the multitudinous bars of amber and rose, the sacred clouds that have no darkness, and only exist to illumine, were seen in fathomless intervals between the solemn and orbed repose of the stone pines, passing to lose themselves in the last, white, blinding lustre of the measureless line where the Campagna melted into the blaze of the sea ... Not in his most daring and dazzling efforts could Turner himself come near it; but you could not at the time have thought of or remembered the work of any other man as having the remotest hue or resemblance of what you saw. Nor am I speaking of what is uncommon or unnatural; there is no climate, no place, and scarcely an hour, in which nature does not exhibit colour which no mortal effort can imitate or approach. For all our artificial pigments are, even when seen under the same circumstances, dead and lightless beside her living colour; the green of a growing leaf, the scarlet of a fresh flower, no art nor expedient can reach; but in addition to this, nature exhibits her hues under an intensity of sunlight which trebles their brilliancy; while the painter, deprived of this splendid aid, works still with what is actually a grey shadow compared with the force of nature's colour. Take a blade of grass and a scarlet flower, and place them so as to receive sunlight beside the brightest canvas that ever left Turner's easel, and the picture will be extinguished. So far from outfacing nature, he does not, as far as mere vividness of colour goes, one half reach her.[39]

This is the kind of spectacularly descriptive writing that astonished Ruskin's first readers. But it is not just a piece of exhilarating prose. Ruskin presents nature as a religious text, offering its readers an apocalyptic revelation. He reminds us, in his reference to the 'golden floor of heaven', of the book of Revelation ('the street of the city was pure gold, as it were transparent glass'),[40] and in the 'purple, and crimson and scarlet, like the curtains of God's tabernacle', he alludes to Solomon building the temple in Jerusalem ('And he made the vail of blue, and purple, and crimson, and fine linen, and wrought cherubims thereon').[41] Biblical knowledge was very much more widespread among the Victorians than in our own culture, and few readers, Evangelical or not, would have missed the scriptural resonances that Ruskin perceives in this sacred landscape. What really matters is that we should see the connections in the Bible and in nature for ourselves. 'Take a blade of grass and a scarlet flower' – the passage culminates, as such passages in the first volume of *Modern Painters* often do, with a simple instruction. Whether or not we follow it literally, we perform the act in our own minds, and we trace the arc of Ruskin's own experience. This is what Ruskin means by teaching. Like Wordsworth, he is not willing to speak from a position of authority in relation to a passive readership. He is concerned with knowledge as Newman defines it, 'a state or condition of mind', and in *Modern Painters* he is not generally willing to provide an ordered assembly of facts, or precepts, for our instruction (though he will from time to time do us this service). What he will attempt instead is to suggest how we might enter the unlimited reality that he describes – entangled, mixed, fathomless. 'No mortal effort' can imitate such richness. Here is the divinely sanctioned natural truth that was Ruskin's teacher, and Turner's, and could, he tells us, be ours too.

Ruskin is less brusque and very much more scholarly than Hughes, but he is sometimes just as idiosyncratic in his approach to formal learning. In 1849, still working on *Modern Painters*, he contemplated the possibility of writing an essay to be entitled 'The Uses of Ignorance'. 'One only feels as one should when one does not know much about the matter', as he remarked, only half-jokingly, years later.[42] His chapter on the Roman Renaissance, in the third volume of *The Stones of Venice* (1853), expands the point with more care. Ruskin's account of Venice turns on a celebration of the energy of Gothic, which represents, he claims, a creative experience that was lost amidst the formalities of the Renaissance:

And the desperate evil of the whole Renaissance system is, that all idea of measure is therein forgotten, that knowledge is thought the one and the only good, and it is never inquired whether men are vivified by it or paralyzed. Let us leave figures. The reader may not believe the analogy I have been pressing so far; but let him consider the subject in itself, let him examine the effect of knowledge in his own heart, and see whether the trees of knowledge and of life are one now, any more than in Paradise. He must feel that the real animating power of knowledge is only in the moment of its being first received, when it fills us with wonder and joy; a joy for which, observe, the previous ignorance is just as necessary as the present knowledge. That man is always happy who is in the presence of something which he cannot know to the full, which he is always going on to know. This is the necessary condition of a finite creature with divinely rooted and divinely directed intelligence; this, therefore, its happy state,– but observe, a state, not of triumph or joy in what it knows, but of joy rather in the continual discovery, of new ignorance, continual self-abasement, continual astonishment. Once thoroughly our own, the knowledge ceases to give us pleasure. It may be practically useful to us, it may be good for others, or good for usury to obtain more; but, in itself, once let it be thoroughly familiar, and it is dead, the wonder is gone from it, and all the fine colour which it had when first we drew it up out of the infinite sea. And what does it matter how much or how little of it we have laid aside, when our only enjoyment is still in the casting of that deep sea line? What does it matter? Nay, in one respect, it matters much, and not to our advantage. For one effect of knowledge is to deaden the force of the imagination and the original energy of the whole man: under the weight of his knowledge he cannot move so lightly as in the days of his simplicity. The pack-horse is furnished for the journey, the war-horse is armed for war; but the freedom of the field and the lightness of the limb are lost for both. Knowledge is, at best, the pilgrim's burden or the soldier's panoply, often a weariness to them both; and the Renaissance knowledge is like the Renaissance armour of plate, binding and cramping the human form; while all good knowledge is like the crusader's chain mail, which throws itself into folds with the body, yet it is rarely so forged as that the clasps and rivets do not gall us. All men feel this, though they do not think of it, nor reason out its consequences. They look back to the days of childhood as of greatest happiness, because those were the days of greatest wonder, greatest simplicity, and most vigorous imagination. And the whole difference between a man of genius and other men, it has been said a thousand times, and most truly, is that the first remains in great part a child, seeing with the large eyes of children, in perpetual wonder, not conscious of much knowledge – conscious, rather, of infinite ignorance, and yet infinite power; a fountain of eternal admiration, delight, and creative force within him, meeting the ocean of visible and governable things around him.[43]

When this was published, Ruskin was as far from Newman's theological position as it was possible to be, for this was the period when his Protestantism was at its most fervent. Yet his position has much in common with Newman's thoughts on a liberal education. Both men are hostile to the idea that education consists in the acquisition of knowledge, conceived as a body of information. Both claim that education depends on the active engagement of the student. Most crucially, they insist that learning depends on humility. This is the real point of Ruskin's paradoxical praise of 'infinite ignorance' – an odd moment in his career as one of the most learned writers of his generation, in the midst of a book that consists largely of the presentation of an orderly catalogue of precisely measured architectural observations. Knowledge is valuable, as Ruskin understands very well. But ignorance allows for the understanding that we cannot know everything, and that the accomplished learning in which the needy and demanding self takes so much pride is a small thing in relation to what we do not know, and can never know.

Elizabeth Sewell, Thomas Arnold, Thomas Hughes, John Henry Newman and John Ruskin do not represent anything approaching a consistent body of pedagogic theory. However, they do share crucial points of reference. They are all convinced that the growth

73

into maturity cannot be precisely measured or controlled, for the pupil's uncertain movement towards understanding is not to be contained within any educator's formal criteria. Success is only possible if failure is allowable. In defining the creativity of Gothic ornament in *The Stones of Venice*, Ruskin speaks of the values that govern his understanding of what education can do. The perfection, or even the final greatness of the product, is not the proper object of its work. What Ruskin wants is the kindling of each individual intelligence, whatever its nature, or however imperfect the outcome may be. Here Ruskin celebrates the roughness of Gothic architecture because it is a creative expression of Christian faith, just as education, as he sees it, is grounded in the noble humility of Christianity. Whether or not we share his religion, we can share his ideal:

> We have, with Christianity, recognised the individual value of every soul; and there is no intelligence so feeble but that its single ray may in some sort contribute to the general light. This is the glory of Gothic architecture, that every jot and tittle, every point and niche of it, affords room, fuel, and focus for individual fire. But you cease to acknowledge this, and you refuse to accept the help of the lesser mind, if you require the work to be all executed in a great manner. Your business is to think out all of it nobly, to dictate the expression of it as far as your dictation can assist the less elevated intelligence; then to leave this, aided and taught as far as may be, to its own simple act and effort; and to rejoice in its simplicity if not in its power, and in its vitality if not in its science.[44]

Those Victorians whose writing engages most urgently with the relation between religion and education were not much concerned with doctrinal instruction, or sectarian affiliation. Their definitions of a vital education allow for a connection between the disciplines of learning and the growth of the imagination. What is to be imagined is a larger world than the ambitions of any particular social group can suggest. This sense of relative value is, at the deepest level, what they see as the religious element in a serious education – not the dissemination of a theological point of view, but recognition that simple

74

self-interest cannot nourish the needs of the intellect. Education, understood in these terms, can never just be a matter of vocational training, or the accumulation of facts, though it is inevitably and sometimes properly concerned with those aims. Its purpose is to enrich the mind, by leading it to acknowledge human and natural realities beyond its immediate interests. What remains valuable in such thinking is the sense that the responsibilities of education cannot be fully discharged within the boundaries of prescriptive regulation.

Chapter 3

Teaching Women

Gender and Education

Questions about religion, gender and class collided within Victorian thinking about education. This resulted in a confusion of values. Definitions of qualities that matter for everyone were confined to social categories (like that of the Christian gentleman), creating damaging divisions within educational policies. These were particularly evident in prevailing constructions of gender. The identification of men with the demands of competitive struggle dictated the ways in which masculinity and education were linked. Because women were thought to represent sympathy rather than rivalry, the cultivation of private virtue rather than public achievement was judged to be what mattered most in their schooling. The artificiality of these patterns was not easy to spot for those who were caught up in them. They seemed an expression of nature. As a result, Victorians would often consider the role of gender in education within a conceptual framework that feels very distant from our own beliefs. To understand their perceptions, we must be alert to historical circumstances which have sometimes obscured our view.

Some women chose to accept assumptions about the distinctively emotional nature of femininity, using them for their own purposes as they modified the paradigms of education. Others sturdily resisted such notions, wanting a different kind of freedom for their own purposes. These conflicts were not only of interest to women. Male writers would also take advantage of the possibilities for resistance that women's situation could offer. We have seen how Dickens's ideal of a feminized model for education was based on the supposed domesticity of women.[1] It was an ideal that bound women to the home while it asserted their moral and imaginative authority. Ruskin provides another example of this perspective. His remarks on women in 'Of Queens' Gardens' (1865), subsequently notorious as an expression of male oppression, in fact reflect a divided body of thought.[2] On the one hand, he is inclined to limit women to the role of wives and mothers; on the other, he is entirely on their side, and identifies with the redemptive functions that he believes to be grounded in the home. When Ruskin speaks of the right way of educating girls in 'Of Queens' Gardens', he is not just thinking of girls. He is thinking of himself. Still more deeply, he is thinking of what is best in all human education. Like Carlyle, Ruskin sees a creative reading of history as essential:

> It is of little consequence how many positions of cities she knows, or how many dates of events, or names of celebrated persons – it is not the object of education to turn the woman into a dictionary; but it is deeply necessary that she should be taught to enter with her whole personality into the history she reads; to picture the passages of it vitally in her own bright imagination; to apprehend, with her fine instincts, the pathetic circumstances and dramatic relations, which the historian too often only eclipses by his reasoning, and disconnects by his arrangement: it is for her to trace the hidden equities of divine reward, and catch sight, through the darkness, of the fateful threads of woven fire that connect error with retribution.[3]

For Ruskin, effective teaching for girls is not a question of turning them into refined ladies. It is a matter of enabling them to make the connections, moral and political, that the reasoning of the male historian has obscured. Seen in this way, the education of women is not a peripheral concern. Ruskin advocates an integrated vision

that should be the aim of all education, for boys and girls alike. It is
an appeal for reform, but it is also a self-reflective ideal, for this
undivided sensibility is always the final objective of his own work
as a historian and critic.

Ruskin and Dickens gave feminized ideals of education an
unexpectedly central role in their polemics. Support from such
powerful men was a source of additional authority for female educators. Nevertheless, a generation of active women was not content
for celebrated male sages to prescribe their responsibilities for them.
They were involved in educational activities themselves, and held
decisive views on their purposes. These women often distanced
themselves from the more conservative implications of the arguments
put forward by Ruskin and Dickens. This was partly because teaching offered women opportunities for economic self-determination,
while enabling them to propose independent models of thinking to
their pupils.[4] Women would often encourage their charges to take
themselves more seriously, and this would sometimes mean finding
fulfilment in roles other than marriage and motherhood. The increasing scope for female employment outside the home made these
alternatives more accessible. However, the fact that women were
beginning to chafe against the constraints of the family did not always
mean they were ready to abandon their nurturing roles. These
tensions shape their thinking about teaching. If learning was to be a
matter of feeling alongside knowing, and as deeply involved with
the authenticity of the self as with the confirmation of a social role,
then the cultural identity of women pointed to ways in which
different kinds of education might be developed. Their experiences
in the home continued to favour a personal model for teaching girls,
which co-existed with the drive towards a nationally instituted
system for education. The values that supported this feminine ideal
were often stubbornly resistant to the competitive regulation that
came to dominate boys' schooling. This scepticism sometimes
restricted women's public profile, but it could also help to endorse
their cultural influence. Education is a political process, in the widest
sense, and this is sharply true of its consequences for women. In this

chapter, I want to investigate some of the complex interactions within the work of Victorian women who taught, and wrote about teaching. Their thinking still has much to offer.

A Generation of Schoolmistresses

From the point of view of women's professional achievements, it has been conventional to define female educationalists as a determined group of pioneers forcing their way into heavily defended masculine territories.[5] Historians note a steady move forward from small boarding schools for ladies to the large and competent public institutions that had formalized educational status for women by the end of the nineteenth century, and they generally regard this shift as a thoroughly good thing. Intelligent women, however, saw a more complicated picture from the first. Jane Austen provides a familiar fictional example of a traditional girls' school in the early years of the nineteenth century in Mrs Goddard's establishment, attended by Harriet Smith, as it is described and gently mocked in *Emma* (1816): 'a real, honest, old-fashioned Boarding-school, where a reasonable quantity of accomplishments were sold at a reasonable price, and where girls might be sent to be out of the way and scramble themselves into a little education, without any danger of coming back prodigies.'[6] Austen's tone here is indulgent, for at heart she approves of the motherly Mrs Goddard: 'she had an ample house and garden, gave the children plenty of wholesome food, let them run about a good deal in the summer, and in winter dressed their chilblains with her own hands.'[7] What Austen commends is the school's honesty. It is Emma Woodhouse, and not Mrs Goddard, who teaches Harriet Smith to deceive herself. Mrs Goddard's girls are, Austen suggests, not so much taught as self-taught – they 'scramble themselves into a little education'. Their learning will not be impressive, but it will be authentic. She speaks with scorn about schools with grander ambitions – 'which professed, in long sentences of refined nonsense, to combine liberal acquirements with elegant morality upon new principles and new systems – and where young ladies for enormous pay might be screwed out of health and into vanity'.[8] Like many of the Victorian writers who came after her, Austen has no time for education conducted upon the principles of system and self-interest.

In general it is the triviality of many girls' schools before 1870 that is lamented, in the fiction of the period and in wider debates about female education. The emphasis on polishing pupils for the marriage market, rather than providing serious intellectual or moral training, is deplored again and again. Miss Pinkerton's petty academy in Thackeray's *Vanity Fair* is a memorable fictional example, or the institution that George Eliot satirized in Mrs Lemon's fashionable school for young ladies in *Middlemarch*, where the world of provincial education for girls in the 1820s is sardonically recalled: 'the teaching included all that was demanded in the accomplished female – even to extras, such as the getting in and out of a carriage.'[9] The transmission of social gentility was often a priority in middle-class schools, for both girls and boys. Such establishments were swept away by a tide of professionalized reform after 1870, to be replaced by endowed girls' schools with serious academic ambitions, alongside effective state-supported educational provision for both girls and boys. This movement was an important step towards the wider opportunities available for women today, creating the circumstances which allow girls to compete with and often outperform their male peers.

Clearly, women had much to gain from these changes. The larger schools that grew up after 1870 came to offer an intellectual training that had previously been unknown to girls, of a kind that was later emulated by selective state-funded schools. Newly established colleges offering higher education for women were able to recruit from their pupils. The daughters of the commercial and professional middle classes were not slow to take advantage of these opportunities, and prospects for independent careers for women gradually widened in response to their increasingly confident demands. These were genuine and welcome advances. But the wish to celebrate them has sometimes led us to overlook what was valuable in the thinking of an earlier generation, and might still be important for us, as we think about what large and systematized institutions might lose when set beside smaller and more personal schools. In the 1850s and 1860s we can identify a group of schoolmistresses who were not yet integrated into the public and institutionalized movement for the reform of women's education, and sometimes had no wish to be, but had nevertheless moved some way beyond the simplicities of Jane Austen's Mrs Goddard, the pomposities of Thackeray's Miss Pinkerton, or the vanities of George Eliot's Mrs Lemon. Such teachers were often keenly interested in ideas, and by no means insulated from public controversy. They valued hard work for themselves and for their pupils too. The rewards were intellectual and spiritual, but they were also economic. These were women who were making their own way in the world. Their values and ideologies were often insistently female, and deliberately defiant of the uniformity that gained ground throughout the period. The same could not be said of the larger projects that succeeded their initiatives, where male sponsorship, and frequently male control, became indispensable to the way in which schools were organized.

The 1851 census showed that in that year 67,551 women identified themselves as earning their living as either teachers or governesses (the two terms were at that time interchangeable). They were a large body of educated and economically active women. The census helped to prompt a long debate about the supposed problem of 'spare' women, and it may partly be because of the controversy in the periodicals,[10] and perhaps also because of the memorable fiction of the period, that we have come to presume that most of these women were forced into the profession unwillingly, usually as the result of the failure of fathers, brothers, or husbands to provide financial support. It is easy to think of this group of women as a hapless crew, without much sense of intellectual direction or ambition, generally put-upon, and not usually willing or even especially suited for their work. Marriage, rather than professional commitment, seems to be the real objective of the many women teachers we encounter in the fiction of the period. Fictional representations of predatory governesses on the make, like Thackeray's Becky Sharpe in *Vanity Fair* (1848), or Mary Braddon's murderous Lucy Graham in *Lady Audley's Secret* (1862), are also common. Occasionally fiction throws up spectacularly malevolent women teachers, like the evil French governess Madame de la Rougierre in Sheridan Le Fanu's *Uncle Silas* (1864), with her 'bleached and sallow skin, her hollow jaws ... a steady cunning eye, and a stern smile'.[11] Undoubtedly there were women who fell into all these categories, though perhaps not all that many who resembled Lucy Graham or Madame de la Rougierre. Yet there is evidence to suggest that they were not as numerous as we have been ready to assume. Not every female teacher or governess saw her work as an oppressive fate brought about by unforeseen disaster in the family, to be avoided if possible, or to be fled at the earliest opportunity. Recent research has shown that large numbers of women consciously chose to prepare themselves for teaching, and significant numbers recorded that they had turned down offers of marriage because of their commitment to their work as teachers.[12] Others have left records of their relish for the challenges of the profession, and the scope for authority and influence that it provided. Some clearly did find the work oppressive, but the overall picture is mixed, and often surprisingly positive.

Many of these women taught in small schools, rather than working as private governesses. The schools that they were involved with were sometimes, though not always, intellectually ambitious. Margaret Bell's Winnington Hall, an important influence on John Ruskin, was an example of a consciously progressive establishment for middle-class girls.[13] Some were surprisingly expensive. Fees for a boarding school with a high reputation could amount to three times the annual salary of a family governess. A more modest day school might charge twenty pounds a year, or less. They were often run by small groups of women. Groups of sisters in charge of schools were common – like the Byerly sisters, who managed an excellent school at Stratford on Avon, where the young Elizabeth Gaskell was an eager and successful pupil.[14] Aunt/niece combinations were also frequent; so were mother/daughter partnerships, like that between

Frances Rossetti and her daughter Christina, who briefly ran a school together in Somerset. Partnerships with no family connection were also widespread, and often longstanding.

Given luck and skill, it was possible to earn enough to maintain a respectable household in this way, though such women were never likely to become wealthy. But the proprietors of these schools often understood their work to be more than a way to financial independence. Some saw the teaching vocation as primarily religious. They were training children for eternity. Others were more down-to-earth, wanting to prepare girls to cope better with this world – though some element of religious training was expected by parents, and was rarely absent. The curricula offered in the schools were often challenging, including Latin or even Greek, some serious science and mathematics, history, at least one modern language, geography, music, painting, and scriptural study. The more enterprising teachers would sometimes supplement their income by writing and publishing their own textbooks; variable in quality, but often vigorous and coherent. Because they were not obliged to concentrate on the classics and mathematics, the liveliest of these schools were in a position to offer girls a more stimulating range of subjects than was available to their brothers. Tom Tulliver's dreary experiences with his clerical tutor Mr Stelling in George Eliot's *The Mill on the Floss* (1860) serve as a fictional reminder of what could go wrong for boys, and what the best of girls' schooling was in a position to avoid:

'You feel no interest in what you're doing, sir,' Mr Stelling would say, and the reproach was painfully true. Tom had never found any difficulty in discerning a pointer from a setter, when once he had been told the distinction, and his perceptive powers were not at all deficient. I fancy they were quite as strong as those of the Rev. Mr Stelling; for Tom could predict with accuracy what number of horses were cantering behind him, he could throw a stone right into the centre of a given ripple, he could guess to a fraction how many lengths of his stick it would take to reach across the playground, and could draw almost perfect squares on his slate without any measurement. But Mr Stelling took no note of these things; he only

83

observed that Tom's faculties failed him before the abstractions hid-
eously symbolized to him in the pages of the Eton Grammar, and that
he was in a state bordering on idiocy with regard to the demonstration
that two given triangles must be equal, though he could discern with
great promptitude and certainty the fact that they *were* equal. Whence
Mr Stelling concluded that Tom's brain, being peculiarly impervious
to etymology and demonstrations, was peculiarly in need of being
ploughed and harrowed by these patent implements; it was his
favourite metaphor, that the classics and geometry constituted that
culture of the mind which prepared it for the reception of any
subsequent crop. I say nothing against Mr Stelling's theory; if we are
to have one regimen for all minds, his seems to me as good as any
other. I only know it turned out as uncomfortably for Tom Tulliver as
if he had been plied with cheese in order to remedy a gastric weakness
which prevented him from digesting it.[15]

George Eliot's mordant observation here is echoed throughout
women's educational writing of the period. Trying to impose 'one
regimen for all minds' was, they repeatedly argued, nothing more
than folly. Tom Tulliver suffers from his inappropriately classical
education as keenly as his sister Maggie, who is not sent to school,
and is denied the linguistic training for which she is suited. Both are
the victims of a system that defined the aptitudes of pupils primarily
by their sex and social class, rather than attempting to engage the
individual child on the basis of its relations with the world.

The more dynamic girls' schools in the middle decades of the
Victorian period succeeded in questioning such rigidities. But even
the most effective establishments faced the economic problems of
size. They tended to be modest in scale, often because they had to be
based in the family home. Schools with no more than twenty pupils
were common, and many operated with a dozen, or fewer. It was
hard for their proprietors to lay their hands on the kind of capital that
would have allowed them to operate on a larger scale. Moreover,
many women teachers objected to large schools in principle, arguing
that they could not provide the personalized educational experience
that girls needed. Intimacy might be a pedagogic advantage, but very

small schools were inevitably constrained in the range of lessons they could provide. They were often not long-lived. If a leading teacher left, or the school failed to recruit paying pupils in sufficient numbers, it would close quickly. Some did manage to survive and prosper over decades. More usually, these schools were transient institutions, existing over a period of ten, twenty or at most thirty years. Boys' schools were customarily larger, usually charging higher fees and employing more masters. They were often, though not always, more durable institutions.

However, the fact that such schools were personal and independent, meant that they could foster educational experiments of many different kinds. Their staff had often chosen to train for the challenge. In 1846, the anonymous author of a series of 'Letters to the Industrial Classes' observed that 'The governess now, be it remembered, is a recognized profession, and thousands of young ladies ... are now studying and preparing for the profession, just in the same way as gentlemen study for the church or the bar.'[16] This was an exaggeration. It was not the case that young ladies were studying and preparing in quite the same way that young men were qualifying themselves for the ministry or for legal practice. But there was some truth in the claim. Middle-class women – ladies – were attending the new elementary training colleges, though these were not primarily designed for such women.[17] Others were becoming pupils of more enterprising institutions, specifically designed to train women teachers along progressive lines. Here, as in other areas of educational reform, Continental ideas were important. The Swiss educationalist Johann Heinrich Pestalozzi (1746–1827), with his child-centred model for education, was still a significant influence. So too was the German educational reformer Friedrich Froebel (1782–1852), the originator of the kindergarten movement, whose schemes for the education of younger children were based on the development of structured play, song and creative activities, rather than literacy and numeracy by rote. In Britain, the kindergarten movement was primarily supported by women. Elizabeth Gaskell, George Eliot and Harriet Martineau were all admirers of the early kindergartens. Elizabeth Gaskell persuaded Charles Dickens to publish a favourable account of a kindergarten in *Household Words* in 1855.[18] These pioneering kindergartens were designed to be everything that Thomas Gradgrind's inflexible school in Dickens's *Hard Times* (1854) was not.[19] Dickens's stamp of approval furthered their transition from a social experiment to a more widely approved alternative to heavily regulated systems of instruction for younger children.

Central to many of these models for educational experiment was the assumption that women, fitted by nature for motherhood, were also fitted for the business of education. The German educationalist Bertha Maria von Marenholtz-Buelow, whose *Women's Educational Mission: Being an Explanation of Friedrich Froebel's System of Infant Gardens* (1855) did much to popularize the kindergarten movement, is explicit on the matter. A woman

> should be enabled to take upon herself those responsibilities which men cannot always undertake with actual propriety, and look after those interests which nature expressly intended to be committed to her charge. The position of woman, as mother, nurse and instructress of childhood, embraces the lofty idea of the female sex having been appointed by Providence to be the legitimate support of helpless humanity.[20]

But this could not be simply a matter for instinct. Women must be instructed before they could become educators, and the processes by which teachers were consciously trained became more organized throughout the 1850s and 1860s. The foundation of the Governesses' Benevolent Institution in 1843 provided an important focus for a new sense of collective identity for women teachers, and led directly to the foundation of the Queen's College in London in 1848, an Anglican institution initially established by the reforming clergyman F. D. Maurice to train women teachers. Many of the more progressive teachers of the 1850s and 1860s had direct or indirect contact with Queen's College, which offered teaching by the male staff of its brother institution, King's College, where Maurice was a professor. But Queen's College, which was founded and ruled by men, did not maintain its original enthusiasm for training women teachers, becoming instead a college for the higher education of women in a more general sense. As it became less reformist and more conservative, it grew uncomfortable with the idea that women could be trained for teaching as an independent profession, rather than simply taking it up as a natural expression of their caring dispositions. Even in its earlier and more radical days, not all of the women who were establishing schools for girls were sympathetic to the methods of Queen's College. Some women preferred to go their own way, seeing a kind of insidious despotism in the systems and values represented by the woman-friendly but male-dominated teaching practices of the College. Dorothea Beale, who famously went on to make Cheltenham Ladies' College one of the leading models for successful girls' schools, resigned her job as a mathematics tutor at Queen's College because she felt that it lacked 'womanly influence'.[21] Women who were in charge of their own schools in this period, both the most progressive and the most traditional, were sometimes doing so with consciously separatist motives, arguing that women should themselves be given the responsibility for educating women.

This separatism, however it was inspired, was among the causes of the gradual extinction of this generation of small girls' schools run by women. The trend was increasingly towards larger schools, which were more stable, more efficient, more specialized and more prestigious. The Schools Inquiry Commission of 1864, with its clear identification of the masculine Arnoldian model of the public school as the ideal to which all schools, whether for girls or boys, should eventually aspire, helped to seal the fate of smaller independent girls' schools. The new model was increasingly based on a masculine ideal, from which many girls and not a few teachers felt alienated. It was during the post-1870 period, for instance, that it began to be customary in girls' schools to require masculine dress – collars and ties for the girls, and sometimes, in the early days of large girls' schools, for the teachers too.[22] Men had a growing influence on the organization and finance of these new schools, often serving as sponsors and governors, and they were increasingly inclined to impose their values on the schools' day-to-day practices. The vulnerable feminine tradition that had grown up in the 1850s and 1860s was lost, and often forgotten.

Some of the schools founded in this period did, however, have a distinct and lasting influence. Dorothea Beale's Cheltenham Ladies' College, established in 1853 and still thriving, is a celebrated example. Like the comparably influential North London Collegiate School for Ladies, founded by Frances Buss in 1850, Cheltenham Ladies' College was established on a grander scale than most girls' schools of the period. In later years, this successful school, which was among those institutions whose work Ruskin supported, became part of the developments in women's education that were to supersede the small independent schools of the 1850s and 1860s. But in its early days it had much in common with those foundations. The history of the College is a reminder of the continuities in the history of women's education in the second half of the nineteenth century. Before Dorothea Beale took command, the College had prepared women to be wives and mothers. 'The school intends to provide an education based upon religious principles which, preserving the modesty and gentleness of the female character, should so far cultivate a girl's intellectual powers as to fit her for the discharge of those responsible duties which devolve upon her as a wife, mother and friend, the natural companion and helpmate for men.'[23] But under Miss Beale's guidance, it began to offer middle-class women an education that would enable them to provide for themselves. Writing in 1871, Beale's fellow reformer Frances Buss gave a vivid impression of what drove her aspiration to supply a serious education for girls:

> As I have grown older the terrible sufferings of women of my own class for want of good elementary training have more than ever intensified my earnest desire to lighten ever so little the misery of women brought up 'to be married and taken care of' and left alone

88

in the world destitute. It is impossible for words to express my fixed determination of alleviating this evil – even to the small extent of one neighbourhood only – were it only possible.[24]

The identification of education as a means for preparing middle-class women for financial and emotional independence is a recurrent theme in women's writing of the period.

The crucial point here is that the marginalization which handi-capped women in the middle decades of the nineteenth century also gave them the freedom to experiment. Many of the most successful mid-Victorian women teachers aspired to an education that would combine intellectual training with spiritual and emotional guidance, fitted to the individual potential of pupils. The diversity and some-times the isolation of their work limited its impact, but it was the characteristic refusal of conformity, a resistance resulting from experience and conviction, that distinguished their careers. The schools that they founded have long since vanished, but their ideas retain their vitality. They persist throughout the writing of the period, and are especially resonant in the work of a number of mid-Victorian novelists. In the second part of this chapter, I shall look at a representative body of the fiction that considers the function of teaching and learning in women's lives.

Literary Case Studies

The Educated Heart: Charlotte Brontë

The novels of Charlotte Brontë are closely bound up with the pot-ential for fulfilment through education. Her sense of what it might mean to teach, and to be taught, consistently shapes her represen-tation of the needs of the self. Brontë's engagement with the princi-ples of schooling is in part an autobiographical impulse, grounded in her intensely inward understanding of Romanticism. Though she habitually writes of the orphaned, the exiled and the dispossessed, her novels reflect the history of the exceptionally close and creative family in which she spent her life. But the absence of a mother echoes through her thinking. Her mother, Maria Brontë, died when she was five years old. Remembering that loss, she assimilated the roles of mother, daughter and father within her models for learning, replicating a family dynamic in which the responsibilities of teaching and learning are freely exchanged. One of the most telling ways in which Brontë reflects what is most productive in the thinking of the period lies in her refusal to accept rigid categories of gender within education. Like the Romantic writers who fed her imagination, she locates the growth of understanding within the work of memory, and what she remembers is her own growth to self-determination through submission to a series of hard lessons which finally balance the qualities of masculinity with those of femininity. In her writing, the domestic spaces of education allow for the growth of an uncompromising and complex maturity.

Unlike many of her female contemporaries, Charlotte Brontë did not see the education of women as an exclusively feminized process. It was, for her, always an encounter between the values and experiences of masculinity and femininity. This often made it unexpectedly erotic. Here too Brontë constructs her fiction from the history of her family, for her parents met and fell in love through their work in schools. Patrick Brontë was a successful and extraordinarily enterprising teacher before his ordination as an Anglican clergyman. The son of a poor farmer in County Down in Ireland, he identified the social potential of a schoolmaster's calling very early:

> I shew'd an early fondness for books, and continued at school for several years. – At the age of sixteen, knowing that my Father could afford me no pecuniary aid I began to think of doing something for myself – I therefore opened a public school – and in this line, I continued five or six years; I was then a Tutor in a Gentleman's Family – from which situation I removed to Cambridge, and enter'd St John's College.[25]

The matter-of-fact tone here masks a story of astonishing achievement. Enterprise as a teacher had allowed Patrick to transform himself. Part of his attraction for his future wife Maria Branwell, as the passionately deferential letters she wrote during their courtship make clear, lay in his charismatic authority as 'a guide and instructor'.[26] His eldest surviving daughter identified the world of learning with that of heroic endeavour and strong feeling throughout her life. For Charlotte Brontë, as for Matthew Arnold, this was primarily because teaching was a family business. But it was a business that took a very different form in the Brontës' lives, directed towards private and independent endeavour rather than the development of large-scale institutions like Rugby School, or the educational work of the state. Charlotte Brontë's interpretation of a complete education was always in part an expression of her parents' life together, Maria's quiet and faithful devotion alongside Patrick's indomitable self-assertion.

The important lessons that Frances Crimsworth, or Jane Eyre, or Shirley Keeldar, or Lucy Snowe must learn seem to have little to do with the work of the classroom. This is partly a reflection of the conventional parameters of the genre in which Brontë was working. She was not writing a series of textbooks for use in schools. She was producing narratives of the kind in which 'Reader, I married him' seems a natural conclusion. But her reading of the conventions of romance is a matter of her Romantic and Protestant commitment to the nurture of the individual self, male or female. Brontë recognized that the identities of a teacher might allow women to multiply the definitions of femininity. A woman who had been taught, and went on to teach, could reconcile the passive and the active; she could defer to the authority of the masculine, while claiming much of its power for herself. In her fiction the processes of learning are bound up with the necessary discipline of hidden feeling, but they also have to do with the right to claim a recognized place in the public community. The educated heart exercises powers of self-command, and sometimes of self-renunciation. But it could also control the lives of others. It was in a position to demand the world's respect

91

and even its deference, and it could claim its share of the world's wealth. It was a prospect that many women found attractive.

These perceptions were formed by Charlotte Brontë's memories of her own education. The experiences of the Brontë sisters in the cut-price Clergy Daughters' School in Cowan Bridge in Lancashire have passed into literary legend as the stuff of nightmare. The portrait of the repellent Mr Brocklehurst in *Jane Eyre* has made the Reverend William Carus Wilson, the Evangelical clergyman who founded the school, an unforgettable emblem of male hypocrisy and malice. Biographical work on the Brontë family, notably that of Juliet Barker, has made it clear that the story is not quite so straightforwardly one of exploitation and neglect as we might suppose from *Jane Eyre*'s representation of Lowood, the severe school in which the child Jane suffers so acutely, or from Elizabeth Gaskell's hostile account of the Clergy Daughters' School in her 1857 life of Charlotte Brontë.[27] Nevertheless, the experience of the school and what it had meant, later deepened and complicated by her experiences as a pupil-teacher at Miss Wooler's school at Roe Head, as a private governess and as pupil-teacher in Brussels, was a crucial element in Charlotte Brontë's fiction. Education could lead to personal fulfilment, but it could also be a site of the lonely suffering which Brontë believed to be an indispensable element of growth.

Each of her four novels is directly concerned with women's development through the business of education. Her first book, *The Professor*, completed in 1846 but unpublished until after her death in 1855, is wholly bound up with the world of educational practice, and includes the foundation of what is described as 'one of the most popular' schools in Brussels.[28] Though the male narrator, William Crimsworth, is the professor of the title, the school is the idea of his wife Frances. 'I don't work enough,' she tells her husband.[29] Brontë makes it clear that the success of the school owes as much to her drive and commitment as to her husband's enterprise. In her final incomplete fragment of fiction, 'Emma', dating from 1853, Brontë is still thinking about schools – to the dismay of her new husband, Arthur Bell Nicholls, who recalls his reaction when his wife read the manuscript to him: 'The Critics will accuse you of repetition, as you have again introduced a school.'[30] The story begins with a newly founded school for young ladies, worthy as the narrator tells us, of 'some portion of that respect which seems the fair due of all women who face Life bravely and try to make their own way by their own efforts'.[31] The language here reflects Brontë's own experiences as a young woman without an income. In 1844, the three Brontë sisters, led by Charlotte, had tried to found their own school. It was to be called 'The Misses Brontës' Establishment', designed to provide a lady's education for a limited number of girls who would board at Haworth Parsonage. The Brontë sisters went as far as printing a prospectus,[32] but the plan came to nothing. Prospective pupils might have been put off by the isolation of Haworth, or perhaps by the proposed level of the fees, which at £35 a year plus extras were a little on the high side for what was on offer. This was a price-sensitive market. The Clergy Daughters' school had charged only £14 a year.

The emotional experiences represented by schooling in Charlotte Brontë's work are not separable from the fact that teaching held out the prospect of financial self-determination. Even without the longed-for presence of Monsieur Paul Emanuel, the school he left for Lucy Snowe in *Villette* – 'complete, neat, pleasant'[33] – remains a blessing. Lucy manages her inheritance with energy, and her professional achievement is not seen as a trivial matter in this novel. Like Frances Henri, she is a worker: 'I worked – I worked hard.'[34] But teaching could also offer the potential for sexual fulfilment, as it had for Maria Branwell and Patrick Brontë. When the wilful Shirley Keeldar acknowledges her love for Louis Moore, she does so in terms of the relation between master and pupil that always, for Charlotte Brontë, carries the erotic charge that goes with a woman's submission. It is a moment when Shirley must forget her boldness and consent to be meek: '"Mr Moore," said she, looking with a sweet, open, earnest countenance, "teach me and help me to be good."'[35] In Brontë's fiction, women must learn to channel the current of feeling, and her representation of schooling often serves as a metaphor for the internally disciplined progress of an emotional life. To be taught is to experience the direction of the will as well as of the mind, and for Brontë the culmination of the process lies in the recognition of a life's partner. Charlotte Brontë's fiction is unusually explicit about the emotional hunger that might generate a desire for education, in both men and women.

Villette, Charlotte Brontë's last complete novel, shows how the male professor's work may be supplanted by that of the female teacher. Lucy Snowe's school, both a home and a business, is provided by her lover, and the parlour at its heart is suffused with sexual happiness:

> Opening an inner door, M. Paul disclosed a parlour, or salon – very tiny, but I thought, very pretty. Its delicate walls were tinged like a blush; its floor was waxed; a square of brilliant carpet covered its centre; its small round table shone like the mirror over its hearth; there was a little couch, a little chiffonnière, the half-open, crimson-silk door of which showed porcelain on the shelves; there was a French clock, a lamp; there were ornaments in biscuit china; the recess of the single ample window was filled with a green stand, bearing three green flower-pots, each filled with a fine plant glowing in bloom; in one corner appeared a guéridon with a marble top, and upon it a work-box, and a glass filled with violets in water. The lattice of this room was open; the outer air breathing through, gave freshness, the sweet violets lent fragrance.[36]

This must surely count as the most vividly eroticised school in Victorian fiction. The lovers' commitment grows from their recognition of a mutual integrity. M. Paul's self-determination reflects Lucy's own: 'He was born honest, and not false – artless, and not cunning – a freeman, and not a slave.'[37] But the reader is denied the gratification of a final union, as M. Paul fails to return from his sea voyage, and he is presumed drowned. His courage is acknowledged, but it cannot guarantee a shared contentment with Lucy. She goes on to govern her school successfully, but she must govern it alone. Given the traditional satisfactions of romance, generously supplied in the weddings of Brontë's earlier novels, this is disconcerting. Self-realization is no guarantee of good fortune – a hard lesson for Lucy, and those who read about her, but a salutary one. What her identity as a teacher represents to the reader does not rest on her being a good mother, or lover, or wife, or sister, for she is none of those things. Lucy's story must count among the most stringent expressions of pedagogic self-sufficiency in the writing of the period.

Teaching Independence: Ellen Wood

The need to secure financial and emotional independence was a persistent concern among women who wrote about education in the middle decades of the nineteenth century. Some, like Charlotte Brontë, wrote from personal knowledge. But not all of the female novelists who wrote about teaching as a way in which women could remake their lives had professional experience of schools. Ellen Wood, who did not, was nevertheless keenly interested in what the career of a schoolmistress could offer an enterprising woman. Better known as Mrs Henry Wood, the author of the celebrated sensation novel *East Lynne* (1861), Ellen Wood was of the same generation as Charlotte Brontë. Born in 1816, she was just two years younger. But Brontë had been dead for five years before financial need prompted Wood to produce her first novel in 1860, and her fiction contributes to these debates at a later point in their development.

In 1862, the year after the spectacularly successful appearance of *East Lynne*, Wood published *Mrs Halliburton's Troubles*. Jane Halliburton is the inexperienced daughter of a poor but virtuous clergyman. She marries an equally impoverished and still more vir-tuous teacher. Her husband aspires to be ordained, but the financial and physical strain of providing for his growing family frustrates his ambition. Though he rises to become a professor in the newly founded Anglican King's College in London, he wears himself out in the process, dies early, and leaves his wife and family destitute. He is seen as a weak and unreliable creature, while Jane Halliburton is celebrated as a much more energetic representative of the moral energy of the commercial middle classes. She stalwartly rescues the family from disaster, first by sewing gloves, and then by becoming an independent schoolmistress. Her sons diligently apply themselves to their books, and succeed in reclaiming the family's position – one becomes a thriving businessman, one a lawyer, one a clergyman. All of the novels of Ellen Wood are deeply preoccupied with social class, and this one is particularly so. After the Halliburtons have succeeded in establishing themselves in prosperity, Jane talks to her son Frank:

> Frank was indignant. 'You are not a schoolmistress, mamma. ...'
>
> 'Frank', interrupted Jane, her tone changing to seriousness.
>
> 'What, mamma?'
>
> 'I am *thankful* to be one.'
>
> The tears rose to Frank's eyes. 'You are a *lady*, mamma. I shall never think you anything else. There!'
>
> Jane smiled. 'Well, I hope I am, Frank; although I help to make gloves, and teach boys good English.'[38]

One of the telling features of this edifying story is that Jane the schoolmistress succeeds as an educationalist where her husband the professor had failed. Like Lucy Snowe, though rather more cheerfully, she inherits the vocation of a partner who did not survive. Taking in boarders for the local cathedral school and teaching them in the evening, she is said to earn 'between two and three hundred a year'[39] – perhaps an unrealistically high sum for activity of this kind, though she is unusual in that she is giving serious instruction to boys rather than girls, a service which commanded a premium. But Ellen Wood's story of Jane's triumph over trouble is presented as an aspirational ideal rather than a matter of social record. She is making money through education, and saving her family in the process. She is also handing on her own religious and moral values. Honesty, self-discipline, Christian charity, industry, loyalty are among the lessons she provides, both to her sons and to her pupils. A simpler figure than Lucy Snowe, Jane Halliburton is comparable with Charlotte Brontë's heroine in the reminder she provides that a woman's vital integrity as a teacher might be achieved without a male partner. She survives, and prospers; her husband fails, and dies. Jane, like Lucy, teaches alone. Wood presents Jane Halliburton as an exemplary heroine, though in many ways a conservative one. She is a corrected version of the self-destructive Isabel Vane, whose masochistic invisibility as a tragic governess had so captivated the readers of *East Lynne*. Jane has all of Isabel's courage, and none of her waywardly engaging wilfulness. She is seen primarily as a competent mother, rather than a would-be lover, and it is as a mother that she finds emotional fulfilment. Seen beside Jane Eyre or Lucy Snowe, she is a straightforward and somewhat charmless creature. But like Charlotte Brontë, Wood wishes to teach her readers that sources of learning might be recast within a feminized definition of authority. What she offers her pupils is a modest range of practical skills – accurate reading and writing – rather than the adventures of literature, philosophy, or science. She has no wish to transform their intellectual lives, but limits her ambition to supplying them, and herself, with the means of respectability, security and an income. Yet this quiet ambition has a subversive edge. Though Jane Halliburton remains loyal to the Anglican church, its male traditions are not sufficient for her needs, nor can the newly founded but still very masculine King's College provide for her development. Wood locates the future prosperity of the middle classes in the imaginative enterprise and spiritual independence of its women.

Jane Halliburton's work as a schoolmistress was something different from being a governess in a domestic context, an occupation that was also seen as a legitimate calling for gentlewomen who needed to earn a living through teaching. The private governess's assimilation into another family meant that she was not in a position to support a family of her own, even if the scant income she earned could enable her to do so. Furthermore, her social position was notoriously dubious. She had put her gentility on the market, and was half lady, half domestic servant.[40] As Charlotte Brontë famously and bitterly noted, 'a private governess has no existence, is not considered as a living and rational being except as connected with the wearisome duties she has to fulfil'.[41] It is significant that Jane Halliburton's spirited sister, who has been carefully trained to become a governess, rushes into an unwise marriage rather than consent to such servitude. Ellen Wood, whose thinking about women's position characteristically fuses a measure of social protest with an unwavering conservatism, is at pains to emphasize that Jane's position as an independent schoolmistress is perfectly compatible with her gentility, and can establish a sound foundation for the gentility of her sons. She remains a lady; her sons become gentlemen: ' "I wish", she added earnestly, "that the whole world could learn that same great lesson that I have learnt. I have – I humbly hope I have – been enabled to teach it to my boys. I have tried to do it from their very earliest years." '[42] For all its conformism, this fictional transition from defeated professor to flourishing schoolmistress in *Mrs Halliburton's Troubles* is a significant indication of new models for educational thinking, as they were beginning to influence popular didactic literature like that of Ellen Wood.

Practical Faith: Elizabeth Sewell

One of the most remarkable of those who claimed that a career as a teacher could provide both professional autonomy and a path to emotional maturity for a woman was the novelist and educationalist Elizabeth Sewell. Sewell was born on the Isle of Wight in 1815, and died in 1906. It was a long, productive life. She came from a high-achieving family – Anglican, professional and publicly-minded. There were seven sons and five daughters. The numerous and enterprising brothers, many of whom earned high-profile success in the field of education, dominated her early life, so much so that her brooding and self-examining nature as a girl led to their calling her 'Blighted Betty'. Richard Clarke Sewell became Fellow and Vice-President of Magdalen College in Oxford, and later Reader in Law at Melbourne University in Australia; Henry Sewell became a politician in New Zealand, and eventually its first premier; James Edwards Sewell was a Fellow of New College Oxford and vice-chancellor of the university, while the impulsive William Sewell, the brother that Elizabeth was closest to and the one who gave her most trouble, was a fellow of Exeter College Oxford, and one of the founders of the public school Radley College. But Elizabeth's father, Thomas Sewell, was not the competent patriarchal pillar of this successful family that might have been predicted. Fathers and husbands in Sewell's fiction are almost always financially short-sighted, and often cantankerous. Perhaps something of this kind was true of Thomas Sewell. What is certain is that he died, in 1842, deep in debt. Elizabeth Sewell had no doubt that she should take an active share in paying off the creditors. This she did partly through her literary labour. Her devotional and fictional works, the earliest of them published as having been edited by her brother William, made significant sums of money for the family. But they didn't make enough, and in 1852, with the help of her older sister Ellen Mary, she founded a school.

Elizabeth's school was in many ways characteristic of the small girls' schools established and run by women in the 1840s and 1850s. It was intended to create a version of home. This domesticity, together with her assertive Christianity, has meant that she is usually identified among the more conservative women educators of her generation. Nevertheless, what Sewell had to offer her pupils was deeply serious, and in some significant ways it was progressive. Education was, for her, always a moral process, but moral and religious growth could not take place without the support of a strongly disciplined and well-stocked mind. She insisted on the need for intellectual independence in her pupils, and the development of their powers of reasoning. The curriculum was wide-ranging and, for the most able girls, demanding. It included an emphasis on history, Sewell's own favourite subject, and also offered the opportunity to study Latin, which she considered a valuable pursuit for talented girls. But she also thought it necessary to adapt the syllabus to suit the individual needs and aptitudes of her pupils. Elizabeth Sewell, like Jane Austen, had a lifelong hostility to anything resembling a rigid system for all. In the mid-1860s, she came to feel that the kind of education she was providing in her much-praised school was too exclusive, and should be made available to a wider range of girls. She accordingly opened a second and larger school on the Isle of Wight, later known as St Boniface School. Her posthumously published autobiography (1907) makes it clear that in this enterprise she was influenced by the broader currents of change beginning to make themselves felt in reforming circles – including, for instance, the inspiring example of Frances Buss, whom she particularly admired. The new school catered for less affluent girls, many of them daughters of tenant farmers on the island. The fees were relatively low. Despite its ambitious curriculum, it charged only thirty pounds a year for boarders, which was a bargain in terms of the contemporary educational market. This second school was solidly successful, until the appearance of larger establishments in the later 1880s on the mainland created still more efficient and keenly-priced rivals.

In 1865, just before she opened her new school on the Isle of Wight, Sewell published *Principles of Education*, a two-volume work on educational theory. Its religious tone makes Sewell's Christian priorities clear. But the book is also a business-like guide to running a girls' school. Despite its title, it is sceptical of the whole idea of having any principles for education. 'Principles! The world is weary of principles. What it wants is practice.'[43] Sewell has a profound mistrust of any kind of uniform educational method, for no such scheme could allow for the growth of the individual mind. 'A system, indeed, even supposing it to be good for one, cannot possibly be good for all.'[44] Nor does she have any time for the idealization of education. Generations of schoolgirls had taught her what every practising teacher knows – that the day-to-day exercise of educating young people is, as she puts it, mostly a 'wearing, fretting, unexciting' business; it is, she reminds us, 'no matter of romance'.[45] Sewell goes on to give some very rational advice. One of the themes of the book is the folly of not educating girls for the financial realities of independent life, should they remain unmarried. In many cases, women's education left them unfitted to teach. This was a matter on which Sewell shared the views of Frances Buss. 'Why is it', she asks, 'that so many fathers in the professional ranks – from which the majority of governesses are taken – give little or no thought to their daughters' future maintenance, except so far as it may be secured by marriage?'[46] One of the reasons, she concludes, is the widespread feeling that a sound education might disqualify girls for the marriage market in which their best prospects were assumed to lie. 'The clever woman, who has an opinion of her own, is alarming, more especially if she ventures to strengthen her statement by facts.'[47] Sewell argued that a rigorous and substantial schooling would enable girls to earn a living by teaching others, and teaching them well, should the need or inclination arise. It was a point that many men were reluctant to concede, and for this reason women should, in Sewell's view, take charge of the necessary reform of the education of girls themselves. Under no circumstances should they be tempted to hand over this responsibility to male colleagues, no matter how sympathetically inclined such men might be. Sewell is approving in her mention of Queen's College. But she is among those women who lament the fact that men were in charge of its day-to-day operation. Men, she argues, 'however earnest, devoted, and intellectual, are not the persons whom nature points out as fitted to be the educators of young girls ... Women can deal with women as men never can'.[48]

'Education is too important a matter for theory.'[49] This belief, which runs through Sewell's *Principles of Education,* leads her to make teaching the substance of her fiction as it is of her non-fictional work. She published thirteen novels and three volumes of short stories, alongside numerous devotional and historical books for use in schools. The strongest of the novels date from the 1850s – *The Experience of Life* (1853), *Katharine Ashton* (1854) and *Ursula* (1858).

They represent a sophisticated and vigorous body of fiction. All of Sewell's work, whether or not it was intended for the schoolroom or directly concerned with teaching, enacts the thinking that she articulates in the *Principles of Education*. Women are urged to expand their talents to the full, in the interests of their own self-respect, and for the sake of those who needed their teaching and influence. Over and over again, Sewell's acerbic fiction warns of the dangers of over-dependence on fathers and brothers, who consistently prove themselves to be erratic and irresponsible. There is a discernible autobiographical dimension to this aspect of her writing, especially when it takes the form of warnings against the hero-worship of careless elder brothers. Long after she had redeemed her father's debts, Sewell's life had been burdened with the need to rescue her able but volatile and often irresponsible brothers from their various disasters. Never married herself, she is not much interested in the conventions of romance and courtship. Many of her heroines do not marry. When they do, the process that leads to the altar does not form the central interest of the narrative. One of the most forceful and complex of her female protagonists, Katharine Ashton, speaks about marriage with disconcerting coolness as her own wedding day approaches: 'Nothing better if it is a woman's voluntary choice, and she has had plenty of time to think about it; and nothing worse, if she is forced into it, because it is all she has to look to. I do believe earnestly that one of the things most essential for a woman's good-ness and happiness, is to be independent of marriage.'[50] Unhappy marriages are common in her fiction, and Sewell writes of their miseries with unsettling intensity. She resists the expectations of genre, and is particularly sceptical about the assumptions of romance.

Not all women should marry. But all women, in Sewell's view, should teach. Some would do so in a formal context, working either for families, or for schools. In Sewell's largely autobiographical novel *The Experience of Life*, the sharp-tongued Sally Mortimer rescues her family from financial shipwreck by founding a school, just as Sewell had done. Sally is herself taught to find her strength by an older woman, her aunt Sarah: 'Don't be a burden upon any one: you have head and hands, use them.'[51] Other women would teach their children, young siblings, or other family members, as Margaret Percival is seen to do in Sewell's 1847 novel of that name. Still more would teach in a much broader social setting. It was women's duty, as Sewell sees it, to assume the moral authority that comes with religious understanding. They would teach through the example of their own constantly reiterated courage, patience, generosity and self-discipline. They would be supported by the church, and Sewell's high Anglican sympathies are frequently expressed in her fiction. But they would not allow themselves to be dominated by the church, or by the men of the church. An interesting moment in the autobiography recalls Sewell's reading of a fevered Tractarian novel, *Chollerton: A Tale of our own Times*, published by Cecilia Frances Tilley in 1846.

> I took up *Chollerton* (a Church tale) and skimmed parts through the uncut leaves and was not fascinated … there seemed too much womanish humility. In one place the authoress cannot follow a young clergyman, by description, in his feelings, or intrude 'into that sacred edifice which formerly a woman's foot was forbidden to profane.' This is, if I remember rightly, the drift of the observation, and really my humility cannot reach that depth. I think I can imagine something of what a clergyman might feel, and I should never consider it an intrusion to go wherever men go, taking them as men.[52]

The sharp and sensible tone here is very characteristic of Sewell. Despite her commitment to the Anglican church, she is not at all interested in theological disputes, and is inclined to see good in all faith. Even *Margaret Percival*, supposedly written in part to warn of the dangers of Romanism, has a deeply attractive and indeed saintly Catholic heroine, while the repressive Anglican clergyman who attempts to dominate Margaret's life is very disparagingly presented. Sewell is much more concerned with the mundane duties of Christian charity, exercised within the small community of the family, or the larger one of the neighbourhood. In her novels, virtue and the hope of redemption has much more to do with keeping your temper in the face of the irritations of living with others than with the abstract particularities of ritual, which are generally seen as the product of self-regarding male fuss. For all their religious devotion, Sewell's heroines are rarely seen in church.

Two years after Sewell published *Principles of Education*, she brought out her novels *The Journal of a Home Life* (1867), followed by *After Life* (1868), in which she makes her mature views on education explicit. The heroine of the novels, the unromantic middle-aged widow Mrs Anstruther, finds herself with six children to teach. Her story is in one sense a study in failure. Mrs Anstruther begins with resoundingly confident ideals, sure that she knows exactly what blend of domestic and institutional education is right for her brood. But the children prove to be less tractable, and less knowable, than she had supposed. She makes mistakes, and the outcome of her work is not what she had envisaged.

> ... as I look around, and see the many influences which have united in forming the characters of the children, whom I once fancied I was training according to my own theories, I almost begin to question whether, in fact, I have laboured at all. Certainly I have not done what I intended to do, and the result has not been what I expected. Not one of my children has realised my ideal – and yet I do not say that this ideal would have been better than reality; for I never supposed they would be perfect; I never imagined them gifted with wonderful talents; but I fancied I understood the materials with which I had to deal, and that, by working upon them in certain ways, I should assuredly produce a foreseen and definite result.[53]

This is ruefully honest. But it is more than an admission of defeat, for what Mrs Anstruther is saying is that she, as a teacher, has learned from experience, just as her pupils have. She tells her readers that 'I only know that I seem always to be in a process of formation; always, as it were, receiving into and amalgamating with myself, the residuum of the moral experiments which I am unconsciously making.'[54] This fluid and dynamic reciprocity, in which wisdom is the product of experiment and risk, often of disappointment, lies at the centre of Sewell's educational thought, as of her fiction. At the heart of what Sewell urges is the expansion of the memory, as the primary way of giving the young a sense of their place in the world, and the old the means to confirm it. They should be able to make vital connections between the past and the present, of the kind that the study of history, literature, ancient and modern languages and the natural sciences will enable them to cultivate. This calls for a body of accurate knowledge, and Sewell consistently advocates rigorously structured programmes of factual study. These are essential, but they are not enough. Something more than knowledge is needed to make mature adults of the children who are our responsibility.

Sewell's fiction was widely popular in its day, and sold in substantial numbers throughout the nineteenth century. It is now almost entirely unread, and it is not hard to see why. Her intelligent novels are toughly realistic, often dour, and not in the least inclined to glamorize the suffering that their heroines frequently undergo. The uncompromising didacticism of her fiction has made it unappealing to contemporary taste. Yet it remains a powerful testament to the firm-minded educationalists who prepared the ground for the more secular reformers who were later to build on their work. Sewell used the ideologies of faith to construct fiction that could assert the spiritual and social authority of women. The faith fell away, but the authority remained. Her legacy, and the legacy of the numerous women who shared her sense of pedagogic purpose, challenged the primacy of the competitive educational world that came to dominate girls' schools in the closing decades of the nineteenth century.

'School-Time': George Eliot

George Eliot famously made herself one of the most learned women of the Victorian period. But her sharply divided feelings about what formal teaching could achieve take us to the heart of the issues we have been considering. Her fictional representation of education is partly a question of social observation and satire, to do with a pungent sense of what had been denied her, and also of the limitations of what had been denied. She is consistently sceptical about the benefits of masculine classical and theological studies represented by Oxford and Cambridge. Both class and gender had excluded her from that kind of schooling – as most English men and all women of her period were excluded. Like Ellen Wood, she is not inclined to present university-educated Anglican clergymen in a heroic light. She reveals the narrowness and injustice of the system, while reminding her readers that the benefits offered by such education might not after all be so very valuable. This is part of her work as a politically sophisticated and progressive writer, a woman whose objective it is to analyse and sometimes to condemn the complacencies of cultural life in mid–Victorian England. Her advocation of rigorous and broadly based courses of study for both boys and girls, with a strong practical element, including serious attention to modern languages, science and the traditions of European thought, is one of the most telling ways in which she intervened in the cultural debates of her period. But George Eliot's engagement with processes of education is not simply a matter of political criticism, or even of satire. It also involved questioning the nature of what might be taught, or learned, through the medium of fiction, or more specifically through the development of the realist narrative forms of the novel that were her central concern.

Some of the deepest currents in George Eliot's thinking about education derive from her own experiences. Born as Mary Anne Evans in the English Midlands in 1819, she was well placed to profit from women's growing expertise as schoolmistresses. Though her sex meant that there was no question of her attending a major public school, still less of going to university, she was not wholly an autodidact. Nor, unusually among prominent female writers of her generation, was she educated primarily within a family setting. She was first sent away to school in 1824, at the unusually early age of five. This does not seem to have been a traumatising experience of a kind to be compared with the Brontë girls' joining the austere

Clergy Daughters' School in the same year, but it can hardly have strengthened any sense of unthinking identification with her parents' world. Her teachers confirmed her family's belief in hard work and the possibility of progress, but they also challenged the assumption that women would play a secondary and subservient role within the drive for prosperity, or even eminence. Though the provincial schools she attended as a girl were not intellectual powerhouses, they were ambitious institutions which laid the foundations for the passionate engagement with the life of mind and spirit that was to form her mature fiction. It was at school that her powers were first recognized, and it was there that she learned to take herself seriously. She owed her teachers a great deal.

Mary Anne Evans's friendship with the devout Maria Lewis, principal teacher of Mrs Wallington's boarding school at Nuneaton where she was a pupil between the ages of nine and thirteen, was especially fundamental to her expanding confidence. It was an association that continued for many years, and the surviving correspondence bears witness to its fervour. Maria Lewis's teaching first prompted the Evangelical thoughtfulness that began to separate her from the more conventionally Anglican values of her parents and siblings. The three final years of her formal education, spent at the Miss Franklins' school in Coventry, were less ardent in terms of the emotional and intellectual allegiances they generated. But here too she found that the Baptist beliefs and social aspirations of Rebecca Franklin, the charismatic woman who dominated the school, allowed glimpses of a world richer and more stimulating than the everyday common sense of family life in Griff House.

Both of these schools offered a direct experience of female community, and female authority. As a feature in the life of a young woman who was to become a writer, this was exceptional. The formation of powerful and ambitious literary women in the nineteenth century is often dominated by the example of fathers and brothers. Elizabeth Barrett Browning was encouraged by a proud and protective father. Christina Rossetti is another example, her childhood formed by the presence of her scholarly father, and the collaboration and rivalry of her creative older brothers. Mary Anne Evans's experience was crucially different. Her father was supportive, and he paid for lessons in Italian and German when she came home to take on family responsibilities as a young woman. However, Robert Evans was neither literary nor intellectual, and he did not serve as a model for her ambitions. Later, she came to identify authoritative men like Charles Bray, Herbert Spencer or John Chapman as sponsors of her intellectual growth. But this happened when she had left the experiences of school behind. Charlotte Brontë encountered men in positions of power as a pupil – William Carus Wilson at Cowan Bridge School, or the compelling and finally very desirable Monsieur Heger in Brussels, who was in part the model for *Villette*'s Paul Emanuel. Mary Anne Evans's early learning took place in a more feminine world. Later, the erotic dimension of the interaction between master and pupil that had always figured in Brontë's understanding of education also becomes important to her. But in her life and fiction these relations form outside the institutional schoolroom.

The diverse experiences she had at school were the starting point for the broad and essentially Continental model for learning that she advocated all her life. After the provincial Mary Anne Evans had transformed herself into George Eliot, the *nom-de-plume* she adopted when her first fiction appeared in 1857, she saw the conventional education of middle-class Englishmen as blinkered and parochial. The kind of reform that Thomas Arnold had famously attempted in his work at Rugby School had, as she saw the matter, done little to improve matters. Writing to Harriet Beecher Stowe about the reception of the Jewish element in *Daniel Deronda*, she noted bitterly that:

I find men educated at Rugby supposing that Christ spoke Greek. To my feeling, this deadness to the history which has prepared half our world for us, this inability to find interest in any form of life that is not clad in the same coat-tails and flounces as our own lies close to the worst kind of irreligion. The best that can be said of it is, that it is a sign of the intellectual narrowness – in plain English, the stupidity, which is still the average mark of our culture.[55]

The most culturally prestigious conventions of education were not only hidebound in their Englishness, but also in their religious identity. For all Thomas Arnold's ecumenical instincts, Rugby was an Anglican institution, as were the numerous schools that followed its agenda for reform. Thomas Arnold was an ordained Anglican minister, and an important figure in the Church. Throughout George Eliot's lifetime, most undergraduates at Oxford or Cambridge were destined to become clergymen in the Church of England. In George Eliot's novels, the masculine stupidity that paralyzes scholarship also saps national religion. The weakest and most destructive representatives of the world of learning in her fiction are all clergymen – the Reverend Barton, Mr Stelling, Casaubon.

The schools attended by Mary Anne Evans had certainly not been feminine rivals for Rugby. But she had at least been exposed to modern languages, in a way that was eventually to open the door to European thought, and that was not common among the graduates of Oxford and Cambridge. French, Italian or German were desirable accomplishments in a young woman, while boys were expected to concentrate almost exclusively on Latin and Greek. The most devastating condemnation of the 'intellectual narrowness' resulting from that particular deficiency is to be seen in the pedant Edward Casaubon, whose laborious studies are rendered worthless by his failure to engage with dynamic new thinking emerging from the universities of Germany. It is not an accident that the only young man in her fiction who really profits from a British university education is Christy Garth, son of the idealized Caleb Garth in *Middlemarch*. Christy goes to university in Glasgow, where he encounters a Continental tradition of thought. In *Daniel Deronda*, Daniel's guardian Sir Hugo approves of his charge's interest in European languages as a schoolboy:

> I'm glad you have done some good reading outside your classics, and have got a grip of French and German. The truth is, unless a man can get the prestige and income of a Don and write donnish books, it's hardly worth while for him to make a Greek and Latin machine of

himself and be able to spin out pages of the Greek dramatists at any verse you'll give him as a cue. That's all very fine, but in practical life, nobody does give you the cue for pages of Greek.[56]

That emphasis on the need for the practical, alongside the Continental, is a recurrent theme in George Eliot's work, and it is one of the ways in which the example of her father, the capable estate manager Robert Evans, does leave a positive trace in her work. In *Adam Bede*, Arthur Donnithorne remarks to Mr Irwine: 'I don't think a knowledge of the classics is a pressing want to a country gentleman; as far as I can see, he'd much better have a knowledge of manures ...'[57] Fred Vincy, in *Middlemarch*, does not take the degree that was intended to qualify him as a clergyman, a calling for which he is wholly unsuited. His real education takes place at the hands of Caleb Garth, just as the most useful phase of Tom Tulliver's education begins when he abandons the fruitless classical lessons which are all that the clerical Mr Stelling has to offer him, and begins to earn a living. Here George Eliot's thinking seems clear: a robustly practical education is likely to be productive. Yet even here she is careful to avoid a universal prescription. Education should be tailored to the needs of the child. In the short story *The Lifted Veil*, the sensitive and dreamy Latimer is given a mechanical education, and it profits him as little as Latin grammar suits Tom Tulliver: 'I was very stupid about machines, so I was to be greatly occupied with them ...'.[58]

The practical competence that George Eliot generally favours was not just for boys. It could be as effective in schoolmistresses as it was in schoolmasters. In *Middlemarch*, Susan Garth, Caleb's sturdy wife, supplements the family income by teaching:

She had sometimes taken pupils in a peripatetic fashion, making them follow her about in the kitchen with their book or slate. She thought it good for them to see that she could make an excellent lather while she corrected their blunders 'without looking' – that a woman with her sleeves tucked up above her elbows might know all about the

Subjunctive Mood or the Torrid Zone – that, in short, she might possess 'education' and other good things ending in 'tion', and worthy to be pronounced emphatically, without being a useless doll.'[59]

The tone here is in part comic, and Susan Garth is not altogether a heroine – she is, George Eliot tells us, 'a trifle too emphatic in her resistance to what she held to be follies'.[60] Nevertheless, Susan's approach to the processes of education is seen to be wholesome, and it was one which George Eliot followed when she found herself sharing the responsibility of choosing a school for the sons of George Lewes in 1856. After careful research, Lewes and his partner opted to send the boys to the progressive Hofwyl School near Berne in Switzerland, founded by the philanthropist Emanuel von Fellenberg (1771–1844). Here the education followed the radical teachings of the Swiss educationalist Johann Pestalozzi in combining a strong moral training with the exercise of practical and agricultural skills and the disciplines of scholarship. In the eyes of both Lewes and George Eliot, the experiment of sending the boys abroad in search of a rational and humane education proved successful.

Choosing a school for boys was one thing. The education of girls posed different problems, and here George Eliot enters a debate that ran throughout the years in which she was publishing fiction. She treads carefully and delicately, reluctant as always to be identified as aggressively feminist. Shortly before she began to publish fiction, she addressed the question in her 1855 article, 'Margaret Fuller and Mary Wollstonecraft':

There is a notion commonly entertained among men that an instructed woman, capable of having opinions, is likely to prove an impracticable yoke-fellow, always pulling one way when her husband wants to go the other, oracular in tone, and prone to give curtain lectures on metaphysics. But surely, as far as obstinacy is concerned, your unreasoning animal is the most unmanageable of creatures, where you are not allowed to settle the question by a cudgel, a whip and bridle, or even a string to the leg. For our own part, we

111

see no consistent or commodious medium between the old plan of corporal discipline and that thorough education of women which will make them rational beings in the highest sense of the word.[61]

In *The Mill on the Floss,* the marriage of Mr Tulliver, who chooses an especially stupid wife on the grounds that she will offer him no domestic opposition, is in part an extended fictional demonstration of the destructive wrong-headedness of male anxieties on this score. 'I picked the mother because she wasn't o'er 'cute,' he remarks.[62] Mrs Tulliver is loyal and affectionate, but her feeble-mindedness does her husband real harm. The conciliatory point is that men will profit alongside their wives, if women are thoroughly educated. George Eliot is not prepared to be identified with an oppositional interpretation of the dilemma. A different observation made in the same essay also approaches the question from the point of view of the interests of men:

> Men pay a heavy price for their reluctance to encourage self-help and independent resources in women. The precious meridian years of many a man of genius have to be spent in the toil of routine, that an 'establishment' may be kept up for a woman who can understand none of his secret yearnings, who is fit for nothing but to sit in her drawing-room like a doll-Madonna in her shrine. No matter. Anything is more endurable than to change our established formulae about women, or to run the risk of looking up to our wives instead of looking down on them.[63]

'*Our* wives' – though the explicitly male persona of George Eliot had not come into being when that was written, it is a man's voice that we hear. The point is forcefully repeated in *Middlemarch,* in the portrait of the mutually destructive marriage of Lydgate and Rosamond. Like Mr Tulliver, Lydgate marries an ignorant and wilful woman for the wrong reasons. He too pays a heavy price.

Men suffer, but so of course do women. A defective education blights the lives of many of George Eliot's fictional girls. Their responses are calculated to reveal their moral nature. Gwendolen

Harleth's satisfaction with her superficial schooling is a clear indication of her limitations. George Eliot voices Gwendolen's careless ignorance with the bitingly ironic edge that characterizes much of her writing on education:

> With regard to much in her lot hitherto, she held herself rather hardly dealt with, but as to her 'education' she would have admitted that it left her under no disadvantages. In the schoolroom her quick mind had taken readily that strong starch of unexplained rules and disconnected facts which saves ignorance from any painful sense of limpness; and what remained of all things knowable, she was conscious of being sufficiently acquainted with through novels, plays and poems. About her French and music, the two justifying accomplishments of a young lady, she felt no ground for uneasiness ... .[64]

Such views predict the kind of trouble that lies ahead for the dangerously self-contented Gwendolen.

More thoughtful heroines sense the inadequacies of their training. In *Middlemarch*, Dorothea Brooke is said to have been educated 'on plans at once narrow and promiscuous, first in an English family and afterwards in a Swiss family at Lausanne'.[65] Unlike Gwendolen, Dorothea has the imaginative and moral depth that leaves her hungry for more than this apology for an education has given her. With no experience of formal learning, she is easily seduced by Casaubon's apparently profound scholarship – he offers 'something beyond the shallows of ladies'-school literature'.[66] But Casaubon is a desiccated shadow of what she needs. In a moment of rare self-knowledge, he confesses that he lives 'too much with the dead. My mind is something like the ghost of an ancient, wandering about the world and trying mentally to construct it as it used to be'.[67] Casaubon's melancholy house at the appropriately-named Lowick exposes his dispiriting half-life. Dorothea's boudoir is ominously decorated with images of her husband's faded mind: 'A piece of tapestry over a door ... showed a blue-green world with a pale stag in it. The chairs and tables were thin-legged and easy to upset. It was a room

113

where one might fancy the ghost of a tight-laced lady revisiting the scene of her embroidery.'[68] Dorothea has much to learn and much to teach, but the 'anterooms and winding passages'[69] of her husband's outdated scholarship can only obstruct her education. Moving from her sterile first marriage to a more fruitful union with young and vigorous Will Ladislaw, Dorothea never succeeds in establishing a public role for herself, and this is among the sadnesses of *Middlemarch*. But a muted hint of what might be possible for women is to be found in the novel's history of Mary Garth, who, like her mother Susan, makes her own gentle contribution to the model of domestic education. Mary's husband Fred Vincy, who matures into a worthy man under her influence, becomes a 'theoretic and practical farmer'.[70] That word 'practical' is always a good sign when George Eliot is considering a man's education. When Fred publishes 'a work on the "cultivation of Green Crops and the economy of Cattle-Feeding"',[71] the conservative people of Middlemarch are inclined to give the credit to his wife. But

> when Mary wrote a little book for her boys, called 'Stories of Great Men, taken from Plutarch', and had it printed and published by Gripp & Co., Middlemarch, every one in the town gave credit for the work to Fred, observing that he had been to University, 'where the ancients were studied', and might have been a clergyman if he had chosen.[72]

Mary is one of George Eliot's most effective educators, and in her quiet way she challenges some central cultural assumptions about the nature of gender. But she does her necessary work within the framework of the family, and not in a school. Like Dorothea, and unlike Mary Anne Evans, she has no public career.

George Eliot's divided thinking about the forms of teaching that women need most is a persistent preoccupation in *The Mill on the Floss*. Defects of schooling are clearly among Maggie Tulliver's problems. At an especially bleak moment in her story, she is pitied by the narrator:

114

Poor child! as she leaned her head against the window-frame, with her hands clasped tighter and tighter, and her foot beating the ground, she was as lonely in her trouble as if she had been the only girl in the civilized world of that day, who had come out of her school-life with a soul untrained for inevitable struggles – with no other part of her inherited share in the hard-won treasure of thought, which generations of painful toil have laid up for the race of men, than shreds and patches of feeble literature and false history – with much futile information about Saxon and other kings of doubtful example, but unhappily quite without that knowledge of the irreversible laws within and without her which, governing the habits, becomes morality, and, developing the feelings of submission and dependence, becomes religion.[73]

The dismissal of what Maggie has been taught is characteristically sharp – 'shreds and patches of feeble literature and false history'. Such phrases are echoed elsewhere in George Eliot's fiction. The brief sketch of what education should have provided for Maggie is more interesting, and darker. That knowledge of 'irreversible laws within and without her, which governing the habits, becomes morality and, developing the feelings of submission and dependence, becomes religion' is framed in unexpectedly sombre language. Eliot speaks of government rather than liberation. This is very different from the independence she spoke of in her 1855 essay on Fuller and Wollstonecraft. Maggie has lacked the training that would have strengthened her capacity to deal with life's inevitable struggles. But it is hard to imagine the form that such a moral education might have taken. Even those supposedly sustaining 'treasures of thought' sound peculiarly bleak here – 'hard-won'; earned by 'painful toil'. The passage is a reminder that though George Eliot is consistently hostile to the conventionalities of an Anglican education, with all of its gendered and oppressively class-ridden implications, her own concepts of education remain embedded in the Evangelical thought whose supernatural justifications she has abandoned. The education that would have sustained Maggie is, it seems, grounded in inevitable suffering. In fact this solitary education of the heart is precisely what Maggie gets – and it is what we get, vicariously, in reading of her sorrows and her death.

For all her advocation of educational reform, and she is no hypocrite in urging a more open and rational approach to the whole question, George Eliot has misgivings about the necessarily social or communal aspects of the intellectual life of a school or university. Her own life as a schoolgirl had been isolated, and she had profited from intense relations with individual teachers, rather than the breezy rough-and-tumble of life in the classroom or dormitory. George Eliot's most effective teachers are never seen in front of a class. Mr Tryan teaches Janet Dempster, Dinah Morris teaches Hetty Sorrel, Dorothea Brooke teaches Rosamond Vincy, Daniel Deronda teaches Gwendolen Harleth. This schooling is what Maggie needed, and lacked – motivated by human affection, and leading to self-knowledge and mature action. It is an interiorized form of the education that George Eliot had defined in her 1855 essay on Carlyle:

> It has been well said that the highest aim in education is analogous to the highest aim in mathematics, namely, to obtain not *results* but *powers,* not particular solutions, but the means by which endless solutions may be wrought. He is the most effective educator who aims less at perfecting specific acquirements than at producing that mental condition which renders acquirements easy, and leads to their useful application; who does not seek to make his pupils moral by enjoining particular courses of action, but by bringing into activity the feelings and sympathies that must issue in noble action.[74]

Because this is the kind of teaching that matters most to her, George Eliot is persistently reluctant to show her readers either a school or a university, successful or unsuccessful, in operation. Even Tom Tulliver, whose education provides us with the most detailed picture in George Eliot's fiction of everyday school life, has only Philip Wakem as a strange and detached classmate. We are told something of what Maggie, or Dorothea, or Gwendolen learn at school, and something more of what they do not learn. But we do not see the process in action. Nor do we see what kind of experience Maggie has as a teacher, briefly acting as a governess to Dr Kenn's younger children, and working in a 'third-rate' school.[75] The education that George Eliot cares about happens when her young men and women are alone with the loving but stern voice of a solitary teacher, as we readers are alone with the voice of our uncompromising teacher, in reading of these lessons. Writing to Sara Hennell, she remarked that 'I think "Live and teach" should be a proverb as well as "Live and Learn"'.[76] However, unlike Charlotte Brontë, she had no inclination to keep a school – 'one of the most fluctuating, dubious occupations beneath the changing moon', as she noted in a letter to Maria Lewis.[77] Her business is with those unchanging laws of suffering and morality, which the pedagogic novel can teach.

These complex feelings help to account for George Eliot's notorious reluctance to involve herself actively in public campaigns for better educational practice. With one part of her mind, she does not believe in any educational practice other than that bought by suffering and solitude. In 1869, when the movement for the higher education of women was especially active, she noted that 'It is not likely that any perfect plan for educating women can soon be found.'[78] Imperfection was the point. If patient endurance was the best and most necessary part of education, especially of a woman's education, then procedures that would remove its necessity might after all be a mixed blessing. The capacity for nurturing tenderness that she valued most among human qualities, in men like Daniel Deronda or Silas Marner as well as women like Romola or Dorothea Brooke, might be learned through sympathy and suffering, but no school could teach it. It was especially the province of femininity. She admitted as much in a guarded letter of 1868, addressed to Emily Davies, the spirited reformer and founder of Girton College in Cambridge, confessing that she feared we cannot 'afford to part with that exquisite type of gentleness, tenderness, possible maternity suffusing a woman's being with affectionateness, which makes what we mean by the feminine character'.[79]

117

There is no persuasive suggestion that Maggie Tulliver can be saved, or save others, through the formal processes of education. School is of little use to her, or to her brother. She can only be rescued – if at all – through her quiet attachment to the loving bonds of the past. 'If the past is not to bind us, where can duty lie?' as Maggie asks, in one of the many Wordsworthian moments in this most Wordsworthian of novels.[80] George Eliot's understanding of education is layered, sometimes contradictory. She trusted in its energies. How could she not? They had transformed her life, and enabled her to shape the literary culture of a generation. School had played some part in that, but not the lessons of the schoolroom. The most serious aspects of education, as George Eliot understood them, could not be contained in the experiences of a group. They were a matter of spiritual and emotional discipline, privately borne, resulting in the education of feeling alongside intellect. Daniel Deronda, approaching the turning point of his life, is representative of the need for such an education:

> He was ceasing to care for knowledge – he had no ambition for practice – unless they could both be gathered up into one current with his emotions; and he dreaded, as if it were a dwelling-place of lost souls, that dead anatomy of culture which turns the universe into a mere ceaseless answer to queries, and knows, not everything, but everything else about everything – as if one should be ignorant of nothing concerning the scent of violets except the scent itself for which one had no nostril.[81]

What Daniel is looking for, and eventually finds in the slow discovery of his own identity and place in the world, through his marriage to Mirah and his commitment to the Jewish community, is the imaginative, emotional and intellectual wholeness that fills Lucy Snowe's room with the breath of the outer air, and the fragrance of violets.

The redemptive charity and the power of George Eliot's heroines stem from these Wordsworthian qualities of open sympathy and thought. They are not rebels, and they do not achieve public influence. But it is worth noting that the dynamics of George Eliot's narratives often suggest something very different from the kind of helplessness that characterizes the old Cumberland beggar, or Jo the crossing sweeper. For all their cultural and educational advantages, any man who attempts to constrain or to cheat these powerful women is unlikely to see the final chapter in George Eliot's novels. Their weak hearts give out (Captain Wybrow, or Casaubon). Or they drown, as do Tom Tulliver, Dunstan Cass, Tito or Grandcourt. Maggie Tulliver's death marks an exceptional moment in George Eliot's fiction. Her women are usually survivors, and their resilience has much to do with staying out of the schoolroom that they also need and want to get into. This scepticism is repeated in different ways in the writing of other women with a marked interest in education. The Anglican novelist Charlotte Yonge, or Matthew Arnold's energetic and productive niece Mary Ward, or Elizabeth Barrett Browning all share a tendency to be suspicious of schools and colleges that were run according to masculine principles of deference to the authority of textual study. Aurora Leigh, Barrett Browning's heroic poet, learns from books, but her most valuable discoveries in her father's library are not formally prescribed. Following her own instincts, as Ruskin was to recommend ('Let her loose in the library'),[82] she gradually finds her way to the reading that makes a poet of her:

> The cygnet finds the water, but the man
> Is born in ignorance of his element
> And feels out blind at first ...[83]

Like the woman who wrote her story, Aurora Leigh does not go to school. Elizabeth Barrett Browning distrusted educational institutions, but this was not because she believed that the deflection of women's creative energies into formal learning might annul their sexuality, as Dickens sometimes feared. She considered that the promised rewards were not always worth the price demanded, and wanted to affirm the authority of women outside the regulated world of school and college.

119

Finding the Way

Middle-class Victorian women had diverse experiences of education, and responded in many different ways. Nevertheless, common interests do emerge. It is hardly a surprise to find that women were generally wary of masculine strongholds of learning. For centuries the dominance of male institutions had been among the most significant ways in which they had been routinely excluded from the opportunity to acquire scholarly learning or professional training. What is more unexpected is their complicated and sometimes hostile response to the reform of such traditions. Women's identity was bound up with the values of internally disciplined feeling, and these did not sit easily with the professionally controlled models for educational advance that gained ground throughout the period. Progress of this kind might continue to marginalize them, if for different reasons and in new terms. The serious pursuit of accurate knowledge clearly had much to recommend it, and women were only too glad to leave behind the notion that femininity was best demonstrated by ladylike accomplishments. Nor were they sorry to see the end of the idea that a woman's mental existence was composed exclusively of the emotions, or the search for romantic fulfilment. Opportunities for women to secure the means of economic independence through a rigorous intellectual training were widely welcomed, and rightly so. But the idea that success in large-scale examinations or sporting competitions could be the complete measure of youthful merit was alien to many women's understanding of what the growth of maturity should mean. If the price of admission into educational equality was the acceptance of the very values that had excluded them in the first place, then this wholesale assimilation should be questioned, and perhaps resisted. These misgivings led many women who wrote about education to find shared ground with male writers who were comparably ambivalent about developments in prevailing educational orthodoxies. The grounds of their opposition are still of interest to us, as we look for a way through the educational perplexities to which I shall turn in my final chapter.

120

Chapter 4

New Conversations

Education, Education, Education

Since I became leader of the Labour Party, I have emphasised that education will be a priority for me in government. I have done so because of the fact – increasingly recognised across our society – that our economic success and our social cohesion depend on it. An Age of Achievement is within our grasp – but it depends on an Ethic of Education. That is why in my party conference speech I said that my three priorities for government would be education, education and education.

Those were Tony Blair's words, spoken in December 1996 in Ruskin College, Oxford – an institution whose name remembers the educational passions of the Victorians, and of Ruskin in particular.[1] I quoted Blair's battle cry in the first chapter of this book, and I want to return to it now. It was a priority that attracted wide and lasting support. No one disputes the value of learning in contemporary Britain, and the wish to share its benefits more abundantly unites all who are interested in social reform. I do not want to suggest that the promotion of this ideal throughout the past decade of Labour government has been nothing more than the product of political cynicism. Blair meant what he said, and his administration has been

121

sincere in its attempts to translate his words into action. He was right to claim that learning is the key to economic prosperity, in national and international terms. It underpins social stability, and opens the door to personal opportunity. These facts are fully understood, and they have continued to form the basis of national programmes of action at every level. Billions of pounds are devoted to the purposes of schooling, and politicians, parents and teachers all join in striving for the highest standards. Its reach has been extended with the expansion of state-funded nursery provision. An increase in the statutory leaving age to eighteen is on the way. These have not been wasted years. Much has been achieved, and more is planned, as the stream of fresh initiatives continues. No British child now leaves school without having been the object of a serious and sustained educative effort.

And yet the sense that our educational policies are not working as well as they should persists. Sometimes this anxiety rests on hard and unwelcome evidence. State-sponsored yardsticks (truancy and exclusion rates, the proportion of children achieving competent levels of literacy and numeracy as they leave primary education, or earning a clutch of good examination results in secondary schools) reveal dishearteningly high numbers of failing children. Those who succeed often suffer from relentless and competitive pressure. Not every school is orderly; some are violent. Bullying casts a shadow over many young lives. Boys seem especially alienated from schooling, and often leave without the qualifications and skills they need to cope with the employment market. The most successful schools and universities are still largely populated by the offspring of affluent families. These difficulties, and many others, are endlessly debated, through every conceivable medium. The Labour government is ruefully aware of shortcomings in the British record on education. David Miliband, speaking as both schools minister and a close ally of Tony Blair, summarized the problems in a speech of 2003:

> the bad news is that when it comes to the link between educational achievement and social class, Britain is at the bottom of the league for

industrialised countries. Today, three-quarters of young people born into the top social class get five or more good GCSEs, but the figure for those born at the bottom is less than one-third. We have one of the highest university entry rates in the developed world, but also one of the highest drop-out rates at 16.[2]

Little in that uncomfortable picture has changed since Miliband spoke. I am not going to pretend that this book can offer straightforward solutions, nor do I want to suggest that every educational challenge can be addressed through what happens in the classroom and lecture theatre. Many of our current troubles are the result of stubborn poverty, changing employment patterns, family breakdown, cultural diversities and divisions of many kinds. The most unmanageable obstacles have their origins in the communities that schools and universities serve, and not in the institutions themselves. Nevertheless, schooling remains the most powerful tool in our shared aim of giving children from all backgrounds and with every kind of talent the chance to flourish as they should. This is more than a pious aspiration. It is a need, and it is a duty. We have not yet succeeded in making it happen.

The more clearly we can see the difficulties that confront us, the more likely it is that we shall find our way through them. In the first three chapters of this book, I have considered some of the ways in which our educational thinking reflects, often without our realizing it, patterns of thought that are rooted in the Victorian period. I have looked especially at tensions between liberal and utilitarian concepts of schooling, and their impact on the intricate relations between education and social class, gender and religion. In this final chapter, I want to do two things. Firstly, I will highlight some obstructive leftovers in the legacies of nineteenth-century thought. It will be to our advantage to bear these unhelpful muddles in mind, so that they do not clutter our perceptions of the real issues. Secondly, I want to think about what remains valuable in Victorian models for education. The Victorians believed in the power of education with a passion that makes our own commitment look timorous and lukewarm. They often disagreed about how best to learn and to teach, but they did not differ on the urgent need to do so. And there was a great deal of common ground in the conclusions of those who considered the questions most deeply. Of course, we are not now confronting their situation, nor are we working with nineteenth-century presuppositions or resources. But the insights of Victorian thinkers and reformers can still help us to understand how we might give our own children a more complete and vital education.

False Distinctions

As we have seen, the divisions of class, gender and religion invade the work of education at every level, frequently complicating the issues that ought to concern us most. The influence of social class is particularly pervasive, and has long been so. The Victorians took it for granted that education would be governed by the definitions of class. In general they were not much inclined to see this as a matter for regret, particularly in the earlier decades of the period. The forthright terms in which they define the hierarchies now make us wince – the 'lower orders' at the bottom, the 'upper ten thousand' at the top, with various gradations of the middle classes in between. No one now speaks of the 'the servant class', or would refer to their 'betters', as the Victorians did without embarrassment. We would claim to have moved beyond the notion of education as the means of determining and marking class. In practice, that idea remains much stronger than we choose to admit. The fact that we are mealy-mouthed about the distinctions does not mean that they have disappeared. Parents assume that attending a sought-after school or a fashionable university will be useful to their children primarily because it associates them with privilege. Spirited children from less favoured backgrounds will often turn away from such institutions. They suspect, not altogether mistakenly, that progress gained in that way might involve a betrayal of their own identity. It is not always a lack of opportunity that excludes children from educational ambition. Sometimes it is a loyal reluctance to cast in their lot with those who consider their families and communities to be inherently inferior. From the other side of the fence, those who are propelled into selective establishments for the wrong reasons will not profit from their studies. Children and adolescents are perceptive when it comes to discerning the real values of their families. If they feel that the social dimension of education is what really matters, they will behave accordingly. Carelessness, or anxiety, will be the result. Anxiety is the more damaging. The pressure on families struggling to secure entry to preferred schools and universities is sometimes crushing. In *Culture and Anarchy* (1869), Matthew Arnold observed that 'there are great dangers in cramming little boys of eight or ten and making them compete for an object of great value to their parents'.[3] The hazards in what Arnold described as the exercise of 'cramming and racing little boys for competitive examinations'[4] are still with us. Child-racing is a practice which now includes little girls, who are often a good deal faster, and its range extends far beyond the ages of eight or ten. The burden can seem overwhelming, for both parents and children, and it can blight family life.

The essential question here is one which we have inherited from the Victorians. It turns on a confusion between what education offers to the individual as a means of personal growth, and its contingent but often very visible consequences for social identity and advancement. It is not that families who are unmoved by the cultural advantages of education are for that reason necessarily idle and disaffected, or indifferent to their children's future. Such families are often suspicious of the idea that education can offer a key to that future, which they see in different terms. Nor is it true that those who drive themselves into a frenzy as they try to place children in their chosen institutions are monsters of snobbery, for these families are often keenly aware of the more intangible advantages that might be available in a serious education. What is happening is that both groups are inclined to put the secondary and external characteristics of the process before its actuality for the inner life. In fact, the social and personal purposes of learning are in constant connection, each dependent on the other. The public language in which we try to formulate these questions is often jarringly inadequate, demonstrating the very qualities of alienation (in Marx's helpful early sense of a radical division within energies that should be single and whole) that education has the power to heal. Alan Johnson, in his capacity of Secretary of State for Education and Skills, provides a revealing example in an address to Parliament in March 2007. Attempting a definition of the nature of his job, he claims that 'in the past education was predominantly a matter of social progress with an economic dimension. Now, it is primarily an issue of economic stability with a very important social dimension'.[5] Whatever education might be, it is certain that it is a good deal more than that. Yet Alan Johnson's turn of phrase is wholly typical of his political class. Such language is not capable of responding to the pedagogic issues that matter to our lives. We might remember Matthew Arnold here, as he considered the force of different kinds of language:

> Evidently, if the object be one not fully to be grasped, and one to inspire emotion, the language of figure and feeling will satisfy us better about it, will cover more of what we seek to express, than the language of literal fact and science. The language of science about it will be *below* what we feel to be the truth.[6]

Johnson's terminology is inadequate for precisely this reason. It falls below the nature of the object, and as such it can only obscure the difficulties we confront.

A comparison between the cultural roles of education and religion as they have shifted over the years continues to be helpful, as we try to understand these issues more clearly. For the Victorians, an allegiance to faith would often signal little more than a willingness to conform. Alternatively, it might serve as a support for social ambition. But it also constituted a serious foundation for the lives of many believers, providing them with the publicly authorized 'language of figure and feeling' which we have now lost. As the dominance of the churches has retreated, education has moved into some of

126

the roles previously performed by religion. In this respect, as in the relation between education and social class, the increasingly central role of competitive examinations has helped to define changing patterns of emphasis. In contemporary British society, a collection of solid examination results exhibits cultural obedience alongside competence, rather as regular church attendance used to serve as a demonstration of the kind of compliance that might qualify the worshipper for preferment or employment. This function of the examination system has intensified as the syllabuses of GCSEs, AS levels and A levels have grown more prescriptive, with correspondingly rigid marking schemes allocating the grades that allow access to higher education and well-paid employment. This is one of the areas where it is easier to mock Victorian conformity than to recognize our own. For the most part, success in our examinations is not primarily a matter of independent thought and response, but of continuously maintained application, and a willingness to absorb information and accept authority. This may be one of the reasons for the growing success of girls within the examination structure. Girls are in general expected to behave less boisterously or rebelliously than boys, and often find conventionally feminine models for gaining social approval easier to adapt to the unrelenting demands of the twenty-first-century examinations system. For both girls and boys, examinations have become a ritual point of entry into the adult world. The strain that would sometimes accompany a conscientious middle-class girl's preparation to be confirmed as a communicating member of the church in the mid-Victorian period has an oddly recognizable reflection in her contemporary counterpart's life, as she trains for the procession of SATs, GCSEs, AS levels and A levels that will certify full membership of her social group. Boys, then as now, were more likely to assert their growing independence by developing some degree of distance from these collective processes. There are of course many exceptions to these broad trends, but their general direction is unmistakable. The difficulty, clearly, is that cultural functions of this kind have very little to do with the real intellectual and imaginative wealth that an engaged education can bring to our children.

'To School an Intelligence and Make it a Soul'

It is now widely believed that the quality of our education is guaranteed by competition – pupil must be measured against pupil, school against school, university against university. And yet we all understand that education cannot work entirely in those terms, for it must begin and end within the privacy of the developing mind. The introduction of scrutiny through competition was intended to protect children against the complacency of teachers and schools who had written off their potential too easily, and as such it was a laudable attempt to shield them from neglect. But this builds defeat of a corrosive kind into the process, for the construction of league tables means that there will always be as many losers as winners, as many below-average schools (subsequently shunned by ambitious families) as those that perform better than average. At the same time, constant assessment of children's achievement tries to ensure that at no point do they fall away from a trajectory of sustained success. No risks can be taken. Again, the aim is generous, but the result is impoverishing. Children must encounter the possibility and sometimes the reality of failure before they can know what it means to succeed. This kind of challenge is wholly different from the demoralizing effect of attending a school that has been formally labelled an inferior institution, in which no pupil or teacher could reasonably take pride.

The impact of a personal encounter with difficulty, where public success is not the whole point, has the potential to be more productive than the oppressive anxiety generated by competitive examinations. The idea that private effort cannot be separated from serious learning is woven into the fabric of nineteenth-century thinking about these matters. It was part of a broadly religious interpretation of a world, of a kind that was not necessarily theological or indeed Christian in its grounds, or its ends. Its roots might be Romantic, rather than doctrinal. We have seen something of its importance in Wordsworth's early work, produced when he was not writing as a Christian.[7] John Keats was more actively hostile to the doctrines

128

of Christianity than Wordsworth had been in his youth. And yet Keats's views are comparable with those of Wordsworth. He too argues that a fully realized individuality grows from a vital connection between feeling and thought, of a kind that cannot be painlessly achieved. In a celebrated letter of 1819, the world itself is defined as the school which will make an intelligence something more than an intelligence:

> I can scarcely express what I but dimly perceive, and yet I think I perceive it. That you may judge the more clearly I will put it in the most homely form possible. I will call the *world* a School instituted for the purpose of teaching little children to read. I will call the *Child able to read, the Soul* made from that *School* and its *hornbook*. Do you not see how necessary a World of Pains and troubles is to school an Intelligence and make it a soul? A Place where the heart must feel and suffer in a thousand diverse ways! Not merely is the Heart a Hornbook; it is the Mind's Bible, it is the Mind's experience, it is the teat from which the Mind or intelligence sucks its identity. As various as the Lives of Men are, so various become their Souls, and thus does God make individual beings, Souls, Identical Souls of the sparks of his own essence.[8]

Keats uses religious terms to describe the process of soul-making, defining the heart as the 'Mind's Bible', and the means by which God translates the substance of intelligence into unique and various beings. But this is, he claims, is 'a grander system of salvation' than Christianity, for each intelligence assumes responsibility for its own progress. In Keats's uncompromising account, no external agency, not even that of Christ, can intervene on behalf of the individual soul. Keats looks forward to an essentially modern position, formulated without the supporting structures of orthodox belief.

Keats's vision assimilates the energies of feeling into those of learning, suggesting a design that would later be echoed in Matthew Arnold's post-Romantic definitions of faith: 'Religion is ethics heightened, enkindled, lit up by feeling.'[9] Thought and emotion are not separate in such models for the understanding of human development. In Elizabeth Sewell's Christian novel *The Journal of a Home Life*,[10] one of the young people that Mrs Anstruther is responsible for educating has been damaged by a period in a thoughtlessly fashionable school. The result is that the essential link between thinking and feeling has been broken. The girl's educational experiences have drifted into a muddle of passively received conventionalities: 'she has heard of what will be said, and what will be thought, and what other people do, till she really has very little idea of what she thinks and feels herself. And till I can get at this, and make her get at it also, she will never really be worth anything.'[11] Clearly, the comments of Keats, Arnold and Sewell do not add up to anything approaching a national scheme for education. Nevertheless, a common thread of conviction emerges from their observations, and many like them. These nineteenth-century witnesses point to the need for an education with the power to bring together the layers of human identity – imaginative, intellectual, creative, emotional – into an experience of wholeness, in which the distinctive qualities of every child's individual power can be realized. Such an education cannot readily be measured within the formal assessments of public competition.

The Mechanics of Learning

I have briefly suggested some of the parallels and origins of these ideals in Continental thought, particularly as it developed in the context of German Romanticism.[12] Here the work of Thomas Carlyle was seminal, as he urged the need for the rediscovery of energies that he believed to be stifled by the values of material success. Not every thinker in the early nineteenth century saw the world in Keats's terms, for this was the period when the consequences of the industrial and economic revolutions were becoming pervasive, as Britain transformed itself from a predominantly agricultural nation into a major manufacturing, commercial and imperial power. With this process came the requirement for a more heavily regulated and productive population. Carlyle noted the implications of the change:

> Were we required to characterise this age of ours by any single epithet, we should be tempted to call it, not an Heroical, Devotional, Philosophical, or Moral Age, but, above all others, the Mechanical Age. It is the Age of Machinery, in every outward and inward sense of that word; the age which, with its whole undivided might, forwards, teaches and practises the great art of adapting means to ends. Nothing is now done directly, or by hand; all is by rule and calculated contrivance.[13]

In 'Signs of the Times' (1829), Carlyle argued that this 'art of adapting means to ends' is fatal to education. Teaching according to such precepts has become a process to be controlled as though it were the business of a factory:

> Thus we have machines for Education: Lancastrian machines; Hamiltonian machines; monitors, maps and emblems. Instruction, that mysterious communing of Wisdom with Ignorance, is no longer an indefinable tentative process, requiring a study of individual aptitudes, and a perpetual variation of means and methods, to attain the same end; but a secure, universal, straightforward business, to be conducted in the gross, by proper mechanism, with such intellect as comes to hand.[14]

Carlyle's first extended work was *Sartor Resartus* (1833–4), an idiosyncratic testament to his study of German thought. Among other things, it is a book about learning. Its semi-autobiographical hero, Professor Teufelsdröckh (or 'devil's dung'), thinks bitterly about the stifling education he had experienced as a boy. Carlyle is remembering his own early years at the Scottish Annan Academy, where he had been unhappy:

> 'My Teachers', says he, 'were hide-bound Pedants, without knowledge of man's nature or of boy's; or of aught save their lexicons and quarterly account-books. Innumerable dead Vocables (no dead

131

Language, for they themselves knew no Language) they crammed into us, and called it fostering the growth of mind. How can an inanimate, mechanical Gerund-grinder, the like of whom will, in a subsequent century, be manufactured at Nurnberg out of wood and leather, foster the growth of anything; much more of Mind, which grows, not like a vegetable (by having its roots littered with etymological[15] compost), but like a spirit, by mysterious contact of Spirit; Thought kindling itself at the fire of living Thought?[16]

Carlyle's account of the spiritual crisis that followed Teufelsdröckh's dismal schooling is in part a reflection of his own struggle with depression as he looked for a positive direction for his life. The book's hard-won spiritual affirmation – the 'Everlasting Yea', as he calls it – is a fierce declaration of independence from the laws of mechanical necessity:

Our Life is compassed round with Necessity; yet is the meaning of Life itself no other than Freedom, than Voluntary Force: thus have we a warfare; in the beginning, especially, a hard-fought battle. For the God-given mandate, 'Work thou in Well-doing', lies mysteriously written, in Promethean Prophetic Characters, in our hearts; and leaves us no rest, night or day, till it be deciphered and obeyed; till it burn forth, in our conduct, a visible, acted Gospel of Freedom.[17]

This is hardly a doctrine of immediate practical use in schools, as Carlyle knew very well. The fact is that he had little time for the disciplines of the classroom. For Carlyle (never, admittedly, an easily sociable man), winning the freedom to learn and then to teach meant removing himself from pedagogic institutions. Like many of the Victorian thinkers who were interested in education, he had experience of the day-to-day demands of schooling, for as a young man in search of a living he briefly returned as a teacher of mathematics in the Academy he had so disliked as a pupil. He found the experience of teaching to a prescribed syllabus unbearable, and became a writer instead as soon as he was able. In his view, the real business of learning and teaching was essentially solitary.

As Carlyle understood the matter, this was as true for the under-graduate as the schoolchild. Though he learned a great deal as a student in the university of Edinburgh, it was the books, rather than the tutors, that he remembered with gratitude. Much later, having written books of his own, he found that he too was affectionately remembered in his old university, when the students elected him to the honorary post of Rector. He gave a straightforward account of what he considered to be the foundations of a serious education in his inaugural address:

> And for the rest, in regard to all your studies and readings here, and to whatever you may learn, you are to remember that the object is not particular knowledges, – not that of getting higher, and higher in technical perfections and all that sort of thing. There is a higher aim lying at the rear of all that.[18]

Sketching out the nature of that different aim to the listening students, Carlyle speaks of wisdom, discipline, and – above all – the creativity of art. Here he looks back to his own great Romantic model, Goethe:

> The highest outcome, and most precious of all the fruits that are to spring from this ideal mode of educating, is what Goethe calls Art: – of which I could at present give no definition that would make it clear to you, unless it were clearer already than is likely. Goethe calls it music, painting, poetry: but it is in quite a higher sense than the common one; and a sense in which, I am afraid, most of our painters, poets and music-men would not pass muster.[19]

What Carlyle, in general the advocate of what he calls in this address the 'loyal adherence to fact',[20] means by this higher sense of art is deliberately not made clear. Like Keats, with his tentative words on what he can 'scarcely express', Carlyle withdraws from any precise definition of the creative life. Each student must discover its resources independently, perhaps painfully, as Carlyle had chosen to do. No precise prescription could be of real assistance.

Admiration, Hope and Love

John Ruskin, deeply influenced by Carlyle's sceptical dissidence, brought his own political and aesthetic emphases to these observations.[21] More sympathetic to collaborative models for reform than Carlyle, Ruskin did not altogether share his mentor's view of education as a process that would necessarily be strongest when pursued in solitude. He supported a variety of schools and colleges, and in the School of Drawing at Oxford he founded an educational institution of his own. Learning could be encouraged and nurtured in the right company, and with the right guidance. But Ruskin was resolutely opposed to the idea that its real work could be measured by any formal schemes of assessment. The 'sting of competition and itch of praise',[22] or what Carlyle termed 'getting higher', that would result from such systems could only reinforce the notion that social life is primarily driven by aggressive rivalries, an economic and political doctrine that Ruskin held to be poisonous. Competition, the engine of the free-market economy, is the enemy of life as he understands it. This was a point on which he never compromises, and he makes it repeatedly: 'The highest and first law of the universe – and the other name of life is, therefore, "help". The other name of death is "separation". Government and co-operation are in all things and eternally the laws of life. Anarchy and competition, eternally, and in all things, the laws of death'.[23] Competitive examinations could play no part in a scheme of public education designed on the basis of such a law. Ruskin's utopian vision for the schools that would be founded in association with the Guild of St George, described in *Fors Clavigera*,[24] is explicit in its view of what examinations can and cannot do. Their role is to be very strictly limited:

> This, then, shall be the first condition of what education it may become possible for us to give, that the strength of the youths shall never be strained; and that their best powers shall be developed in each, without competition, though they shall have to pass crucial,

134

but not severe, examinations, attesting clearly to themselves and to other people, not the utmost they can do, but that at least they can do *some* things accurately and well: their own certainty of this being accompanied with the quite as clear and much happier certainty, that there are many other things which they will never be able to do at all.

'The happier certainty?' Yes. A man's happiness consists infinitely more in admiration of the faculties of others than in confidence in his own.[25]

The development of individual capacity will, in Ruskin's model for learning, lead to self-development rather than self-assertion. Carlyle had told the students at Edinburgh that reverence, not pride, is to be the end of education: 'Honour done to those who are greater and better than ourselves; honour distinct from fear. *Ehrfurcht,* the soul of all religion that has ever been among men, or ever will be.'[26] This was a conviction rooted in both religious and Romantic habits of mind. Each of the five volumes of Ruskin's first major work, *Modern Painters* (1843–60), is prefaced by a quotation from Wordsworth's poem *The Excursion* (1814). Throughout his life, Ruskin returned to what he understood to be the poem's central insight:

We live by admiration, hope and love.[27]

He claims this line as his 'literal guide in all education'.[28] In an address delivered to the Mansfield Art Night Class in 1873, he advises the students on how they might most accurately measure their own improvement:

But, without any reference to the opinion of others, and without any chance of partiality in your own, there is one test by which you can all determine the rate of your real progress.

Examine, after every period of renewed industry, how far you have enlarged your faculty of *admiration*.

Consider how much more you can see, to reverence, in the work of masters; and how much more to love, in the work of nature.

This is the only constant and infallible test of progress. That you wonder more at the work of great men, and that you care more for natural objects.

. . .

You may, at least in early years, test accurately your power of doing anything in the least rightly, by your increasing conviction that you never will be able to do it as well as it has been done by others.[29]

This echoes Carlyle; but for Ruskin, the capacity for reverence that he saw as essential for the growth of the mind was not to be stimulated only by human achievement, but also by the 'work of nature'. For this reason, he insisted that natural science, in the sense of the study of material objects of every kind, was to be central in the education of every child. One of the first objectives of *Modern Painters* was to train readers in the close and active study of natural phenomena. This was not simply a prerequisite for learning about art, though in Ruskin's view no art can be properly judged without some such preparation, but of developing a personal understanding of our relations with the world that surrounds us, in all its specificity and strangeness. The love of nature is not a matter of a sentimental liking for decorative scenery, still less the wish to appropriate natural resources for our own gain. It must be grounded in humility, meticulous observation, and veneration. Love for something other than ourselves can be the most effective catalyst for real learning.

In 1853, Ruskin published 'Modern Education', as a polemical appendix to the final volume of *The Stones of Venice*. It is a trenchant attack on the theory and practice of education as Ruskin had experienced it. Though it forms part of a book that exhibits a dazzlingly extensive and rigorously researched body of learning, this short essay is markedly sceptical of the value of scholarship. 'The great leading error of modern times is the mistaking erudition for education.'[30] One result of this error, Ruskin concludes, is that educational systems have consistently over-valued the pursuit of verbal skills. Here too Ruskin follows the thinking of Carlyle, with his dismissal of 'dead Vocables'. Boys of his generation and class were, in Ruskin's argument, compelled to spend too much of their energy on the study of classical languages, at the expense of the active interest they might otherwise have taken in science, art and politics. In making this point, Ruskin is thinking back to his own discomfort as an undergraduate in Oxford in the late 1830s and early 1840s. Like Carlyle in Edinburgh, he had not had a wholly productive time. What he most regretted, in retrospect, was the required emphasis on Latin and Greek texts, while his own inclination lay in the investigation of the natural world, and in drawing:

> Until within the last year or two, the instruction in the physical sciences given at Oxford consisted of a course of twelve or fourteen lectures on the Elements of Mechanics or Pneumatics, and permission to ride out to Shotover with the Professor of Geology. I do not know the specialties of the system pursued in the academies of the Continent; but their practical result is, that unless a man's natural instincts urge him to the pursuit of the physical sciences too strongly to be resisted, he enters into life utterly ignorant of them. I cannot, within my present limits, even so much as count the various directions in which this ignorance does evil. But the main mischief of it is, that it leaves the greater number of men without the natural food which God intended for their intellects. For one man who is fitted for the study of words, fifty are fitted for the study of things, and were intended to have a perpetual, simple, and religious delight in watching the processes, or admiring the creatures, of the natural universe. Deprived of this source of pleasure, nothing is left to them but ambition or dissipation.[31]

Like many of the Victorian thinkers that I have been investigating, Ruskin strenuously objects to the prevalent belief that the application of a system will address all educational needs – if only the right system could be discovered. Every human understanding is distinct and different, and its individuality must be recognized before its potential can be developed. This is true for all classes. The creative force of the individual, and the honour that it should earn, is confined to no single group within society. In making this point, Ruskin integrates

137

the people he is thinking about with the natural world of which they are a part, whose phenomena it is their pleasure and responsibility to observe. Just as different varieties of wood, and stone, and earth each exhibit their own particular qualities to the watchful eye, so do the various kinds of people who are to be taught:

> But the first point to be understood is that the material is as various as the ends; that not only one man is unlike another, but *every* man is essentially different from *every* other, so that no training, no forming, nor informing, will ever make two persons alike in thought or in power. Among all men, whether of the upper or lower orders, the differences are eternal and irreconcilable, between one individual and another, born under absolutely the same circumstances. One man is made of agate, another of oak; one of slate, another of clay. The education of the first is polishing; of the second, seasoning; of the third, rending; of the fourth moulding. It is of no use to season the agate; it is vain to try to polish the slate; but both are fitted, by the qualities they possess, for services in which they may be honoured.
>
> Now the cry for the education of the lower classes, which is heard every day more widely and loudly, is a wise and a sacred cry, provided it be extended into one for the education of *all* classes, with definite respect to the work each man has to do, and the substance of which he is made. But it is a foolish and vain cry, if it be understood, as in the plurality of cases it is meant to be, for the expression of mere craving after knowledge, irrespective of the simple purposes of the life that now is, and blessings of that which is to come.
>
> One great fallacy into which men are apt to fall when they are reasoning on this subject is: that light, as such, is always good; and darkness, as such, always evil. Far from it. Light untempered would be annihilation. It is good to them that sit in darkness and in the shadow of death; but, to those that faint in the wilderness, so also is the shadow of the great rock in a weary land. If the sunshine is good, so also the cloud of the latter rain. Light is only beautiful, only available for life, when it is tempered with shadow; pure light is fearful, and unendurable by humanity. And it is not less ridiculous to say that the light, as such, is good in itself, than to say that the darkness is good in itself. Both are rendered safe, healthy, and useful by the other; the night by the day,

the day by the night; and we could just as easily live without the dawn as without the sunset, so long as we are human. Of the celestial city we are told there shall be 'no night there', and then we shall know even as also we are known: but the night and the mystery have both their service here; and our business is not to strive to turn the night into day, but to be sure that we are as they that watch for the morning.[32]

'So long as we are human': this train of thought, with its sober recognition of the shadows that are inescapable in all human experience, takes us back to the ideas that Ruskin had explored in his thoughts on Renaissance learning, where he had considered the limits of what he calls here the 'mere craving after knowledge'.[33] What Ruskin describes, in his consideration of the needful balance of light and shadow, is comparable with the 'world of pains and troubles' that Keats spoke of, in his letter on what is necessary to school an intelligence, and make it a soul. They are part of the concept of mystery to which Ruskin repeatedly returns – 'fathomless', to use a word that recurs in his writing, and of a kind that we must each experience for ourselves.[34] The point is a simple one, but it cannot be simply made. It is in part what Keats has in mind when he talks about the 'negative capability' that characterizes the artist's mind, 'when a man is capable of being in uncertainties, mysteries, doubts, without any irritable reaching after fact and reason'.[35] 'I can scarcely express what I but dimly perceive' in Keats's words; or, as Carlyle puts it, 'could at present give no definition that would make it clear to you'. George Eliot, firm-minded humanist, recorded a response to her first reading of Darwin's *The Origin of Species* (1859): 'to me the Development theory and all other explanations of processes by which things came to be produce a feeble impression compared with the mystery that lies under the processes.'[36] In her enigmatic novella *The Lifted Veil* (1859), she speaks of the soul's 'absolute ... need of something hidden and uncertain for the maintenance of that doubt and hope and effort which are the breath of its life'.[37] Clarity is precious, but we must acknowledge the limits of human intelligence in order to reach a final maturity.

If this mystery is to be a part of what makes for real learning, it cannot easily figure in the acquisition of knowledge that is to be externally measured and controlled. It has to do with the unpredictability of the developing creativity of children, or of adults, as they absorb both light and darkness into their enlarging experience, and turn it into something that is their own, a uniquely individual contribution to the world's work. Ruskin's most passionate declaration of what this will mean, if we are to make it 'available for life', is developed in the historical context of his account of Venetian architecture. As we have seen, in *The Stones of Venice* (1851–3), he claims that the regulation and classicism of the Renaissance is deadening, and what has been killed is the individualistic vitality of the Gothic building that preceded it. The medieval builders were hardly egalitarian, as Ruskin knew very well. But the rough creativity of their ornamentation, dark and unruly, represents a vitality that has been lost in modern European culture. It is not an energy that can be made safe, or reliable. It has nothing to do with the motivations of competition, for each makes a separate journey in seeking its imaginative rewards. Ruskin's most sustained attempt to define what he means by this journey comes in his account of 'The Nature of Gothic', which lies at the heart of his argument in *The Stones of Venice*. William Morris, who called this chapter 'one of the very few necessary and inevitable utterances of the century',[38] saw that the point was political, in the sense that all thinking about the relation between labour and art is political. 'The Nature of Gothic' became one of the founding texts of British socialism as it gathered momentum in the late nineteenth century. But it has not lost its power as an account of what education might mean, and should mean, for our own century. Ruskin urges us not be afraid of our incapacities, for they are the inevitable signs of a working mind: 'Do what you can, and confess frankly what you are unable to do; neither let your effort be shortened for fear of failure, nor your confession silenced for fear of shame.'[39] It is the wish for perfection that we should fear, for it is here that the classical legacy that gave rise to the Renaissance is at its most insidious:

But the modern English mind has this much in common with that of the Greek, that it intensely desires, in all things, the utmost completion or perfection compatible with their nature. This is a noble character in the abstract, but becomes ignoble when it causes us to forget the relative dignities of that nature itself, and to prefer the perfectness of the lower nature to the imperfection of the higher.... . And therefore, while in all things that we see or do, we are to desire perfection, and strive for it, we are nevertheless not to set the meaner thing, in its narrow accomplishment, above the nobler thing, in its mighty progress; not to esteem smooth minuteness above shattered majesty; not to prefer mean victory to honourable defeat; not to lower the level of our aim, that we may the more surely enjoy the complacency of success. But, above all, in our dealings with the souls of other men, we are to take care how we check, by severe requirement or narrow caution, efforts which might otherwise lead to a noble issue; and, still more, how we withhold our admiration from great excellencies, because they are mingled with rough faults. Now, in the make and nature of every man, however rude or simple, whom we employ in manual labour, there are some powers for better things: some tardy imagination, torpid capacity of emotion, tottering steps of thought, there are, even at the worst; and in most cases it is all our own fault that they are tardy or torpid.... . Understand this clearly; You can teach a man to draw a straight line, and to cut one; to strike a curved line, and to carve it; and to copy and carve any number of given lines or forms, with admirable speed and perfect precision; and you find his work perfect of its kind: but if you ask him to think about any of those forms, to consider if he cannot find any better in his own head, he stops; his execution becomes hesitating; he thinks, and ten to one he thinks wrong; ten to one he makes a mistake in the first touch he gives to his work as a thinking being. But you have made a man of him for all that. He was only a machine before, an animated tool.

And observe, you are put to stern choice in this matter. You must either make a tool of the creature, or a man of him. You cannot make both. Men were not intended to work with the accuracy of tools, to be precise and perfect in all their actions. If you will have that precision out of them, and make their fingers measure degrees like

141

cog-wheels, and their arms strike curves like compasses, you must unhumanize them. All the energy of their spirits must be given to make cogs and compasses of themselves. All their attention and strength must go to the accomplishment of the mean act. ... On the other hand, if you will make a man of the working creature, you cannot make a tool. Let him but begin to imagine, to think, to try to do anything worth doing; and the engine-turned precision is lost at once. Out come all his roughness, all his dulness, all his incapability; shame upon shame, failure upon failure, pause after pause: but out comes the whole majesty of him also; and we know the height of it only when we see the clouds settling upon him. And, whether the clouds be bright or dark, there will be transfiguration behind and within them.[40]

Ruskin identifies this transformative liberty with Christianity. Only Christians, he claims, acknowledge the potential in every human soul. But such an ideal cannot be bound to the purposes of religion, as Ruskin came to recognize after the loss of his Evangelical faith in the late 1850s. The point is that the 'freedom of thought ... which it must be the first aim of all Europe at this day to regain for her children'[41] will not insist on prescriptive or specific programmes of learning, including any theological scheme of belief. Though the imaginative creativity Ruskin wants to see in every life is not simply a practical means to an end, it cannot serve (as religion must) as an end in itself. 'The Nature of Gothic' is not an argument for faith schools.

Ruskin is talking about the vitality of workmen, not the inventiveness of schoolchildren or university students. Yet his plea for the courage that allows the freedom of creative engagement, rather than the security of measured precision, should be central to our understanding of the processes of education, which do not stop at the school gates. No one can function as a machine, producing a stream of perfect outputs, all designed according to an exact rule. Whatever our age, and whatever the nature of our responsibilities, we need the liberty to experiment, to get things wrong, to see where our thoughts might take us. Few people with experience in the classroom would think otherwise, for teachers and examiners have no wish to convert their students into ranks of robots. Yet the cumulative results of our ever-tighter control over what is to be permitted and rewarded in coursework and examinations has the effect of denying the development of the intellectual independence to which we might pay lip-service. Too much is at risk if a wrong turning is taken, and we are more and more inclined to think that our pupils and students cannot be trusted with any real autonomy. With the best and most honourable of intentions, we are trying to make tools of our children. Small wonder, then, that large numbers of them refuse to engage wholeheartedly with the process, or do so in a way which limits their intellectual growth.

This is not a plea for anarchy, for it is only within a context of order that creativity of any kind can flourish. Reading and writing do not develop without the knowledge of vocabulary and grammar; music can only be created if the student has learned something of pitch, rhythm and key; art requires practical experience with materials and techniques. Similarly, the scientific imagination needs a confident understanding of the language of mathematics before it can sense the exhilarating possibilities within physics, chemistry or biology. For many, the creative thinking that Ruskin advocates will not be expressed in the abstraction of words, or music, or scientific logic, but through an expanding relation with the material world. The skilled handling of a pencil is as much an expression of the vitality of thought as a short story or historical essay. Whatever form it might take – and there are countless possibilities – the necessary fundamentals of creative practice are not acquired without applied discipline, from teachers and pupils alike. But we should understand that the acquisition of these skills is not in itself the highest benefit that education can confer, nor are they best practised in an atmosphere of unremitting scrutiny and testing. The self-distrusting students that emerge from an over-rigid programme of assessment and guidance are prone to anxiety and passivity, the worst results of which are already apparent in schools, colleges and universities. Such students look to adults for validation and support in every aspect of their work, for they have never been encouraged to believe that it will be worth taking responsibility for their own progress. They are reluctant to read beyond the immediate demands of their examination syllabuses, for they do not see that such reading will be of the slightest value to them. Worse still, they are vulnerable to the hazards of over-reliance on the internet, which places huge resources at their disposal without giving them the power of active discrimination that would make such information genuinely their own. Difficulties arising from plagiarism among students, often caused by a lack of confidence rather than any conscious intention to cheat, are epidemic in universities and colleges. If a student has never been encouraged to believe that independent thought is likely to satisfy the demands of a formal system of assessment, it is not surprising that the temptation to try to find safety in the work of others can sometimes be overwhelming.

I am hardly alone in making these observations. Nor am I unique in recalling Ruskin's urgent appeals for something better. It is not an accident that Cambridge's Anglia Polytechnic University decided to change its name to Anglia Ruskin University in 2005. Like the founders of Ruskin College, where Tony Blair made the speech with which I began this chapter, the new university was remembering the educational values that Ruskin represents. Ruskin is a hero of my book, and it is part of my purpose to remind my readers of his greatness. But simply recalling Ruskin's thinking will not get us far. This book has tried to suggest that Victorian ideas can give us a clearer understanding of the origins of our present problems, showing how our tangles over education and class, gender and religion took root in the first place. I want to argue that they can serve a still more useful purpose in suggesting ways in which we can begin to extricate ourselves from our difficulties. We need not feel paralysed, helplessly bound to continue in our present direction. The Victorians came to understand that the system of education that they had inherited from their predecessors was restricted in its range and inhibited in its quality. They made many mistakes in their attempts to put things right, but there can be no doubt that what emerged from their reforms was a more generous model than what had gone before. For the first time, those who had been excluded from learning by poverty or gender had a reasonable chance of a serious education. The grip of organized religion on schooling was relaxed, and higher education became more ambitious and accessible. But the price that was paid for their progress was the growing dominance of a systematized approach to education, at the expense of more diverse and personal ways of learning. Our own struggle to make further headway has exacerbated this problem, as we have persisted in the belief that education can be transformed into a process that can be measured, controlled and guaranteed at every point. The need for a national structure remains apparent, but it is also increasingly clear that its processes must co-exist with a flexibility that can make room for the individual pupil. Passionate voices warned Victorian educators of this need, and we should still be listening.

Notes

Preface

1 John Ruskin, *The Works of John Ruskin*, eds. E. T. Cook and Alexander Wedderburn, 39 vols. (London: George Allen, 1903–12), 17.232.
2 John Henry Newman, *A Grammar of Assent*, ed. Nicholas Lash (Notre Dame: University of Notre Dame Press, 1979), p. 274.

Chapter 1   Defining Knowledge

1 Charles Dickens, *Nicholas Nickleby* [1838–9], ed. Paul Schlicke (Oxford: Oxford University Press, 1990), p. 90.
2 Matthew Arnold, *The Popular Education of France*, in *The Complete Prose Works of Matthew Arnold*, ed. R. H. Super, 11 vols. (Ann Arbor: University of Michigan Press, 1960–77), 2.24.
3 Many histories offer useful accounts of this revolution, including Robert Anderson, *British Universities: Past and Present* (London: Hambledon Continuum, 2006); T. W. Bamford, *The Rise of the Public Schools* (London: Nelson, 1967); Pauline Fletcher and Patrick Scott, *Culture and Education in Victorian England* (London: Bucknell University Press, 1990); J. F. C. Harrison, *Learning and Living* (London: Routledge and Kegan Paul, 1961); John Hurt, *Education in Evolution* (London: Hart-Davis, 1971); John Roach, *A History of Secondary Education in England, 1800–1870* (London: Longman, 1986); Sheldon Rothblatt, *The Revolution of the Dons: Cambridge and Society in Victorian England* (London: Faber, 1968); Gillian Sutherland, *Elementary Education in the Nineteenth Century* (London: Historical Association, 1971); Neil J. Smithser, *Social Paralysis and Social Change: British Working-Class Education in the Nineteenth*

Century (Berkeley: University of California Press, 1991); W. B. Stephens, *Education in Britain, 1750–1914*, (New York: St Martins Press, 1998); David Vincent, *Literacy and Popular Culture* (Cambridge: Cambridge University Press, 1989); David Wardle, *English Popular Education 1780–1975* (Cambridge: Cambridge University Press, 1976).

4   Anthony Trollope, *An Autobiography*, eds. Michael Sadleir and Frederick Page, with intro. and notes by P. D. Edwards (Oxford: Oxford University Press, 1980), p. 222.

5   Ibid., p. 217.

6   Ibid., p. 146.

7   Robert Lowe, MP, *Hansard (Commons)*, vol. 165 (1862), column 242.

8   George Eliot, *Middlemarch*, ed. David Carroll (Oxford: Clarendon Press, 1986), p. 825.

9   Thomas Love Peacock, *Headlong Hall and Gryll Grange*, eds. Michael Baron and Michael Slater (Oxford: Oxford University Press, 1987), pp. 185–7.

10   Arnold, *Prose Works*, 11.212.

11   Alfred Tennyson, 'The Princess' (I.57–9), *The Poems of Tennyson*, ed. Christopher Ricks, 3 vols. (Harlow: Longman, 1987), 2.190.

12   Tennyson, 'The Princess' (IV.21–5), *Poems*, 2.232.

13   Tennyson, 'In Memoriam', (I.21–4), *Poems*, 2.317.

14   Tennyson, 'In Memoriam', (CXIV, 1–16), *Poems*, 2.435–6.

15   See Stephen Gill, *Wordsworth and the Victorians* (Oxford: Clarendon Press, 1998).

16   'Mathetes' was the pseudonym of John Wilson (who published as 'Christopher North' in *Blackwood's Magazine*) and Alexander Blair.

17   From *The Friend*, No. 17 (14 December 1809), pp. 257–68; see *The Prose Works of William Wordsworth*, edited by W. J. B. Owen and Jane Worthington Smyser, 3 vols. (Oxford: Clarendon Press, 1974), 2.30.

18   Ibid., 2.30.

19   Ibid., 2.8.

20   Ibid., 2.21.

21   Ibid., 2.23.

22   Wordsworth, 'The Thorn' (65–6), *Lyrical Ballads*, eds. R. L. Brett and A. R. Jones (London: Methuen, 1963), p. 71.

23   Wordsworth, *Lyrical Ballads*, p. 283.

24   Wordsworth, 'The Old Cumberland Beggar' (98–100), *Lyrical Ballads*, pp. 202–3.

25   Ibid., (102–8), p. 203.

26   Ibid., (125), p. 203.

27   Ibid., (140–6), p. 204.

28   Wordsworth, letter to John Wilson, June 1802, in *The Early Letters of William Wordsworth*, ed. Ernest de Selincourt (Oxford: Oxford University Press, 1935), p. 295.

29 William Wordsworth, 'Lines Written a Few Miles Above Tintern Abbey' (94–101), *Lyrical Ballads*, p. 114.

30 John Stuart Mill, *Autobiography*, in *The Collected Works of John Stuart Mill* ed. J. M. Robson, 33 vols. (Toronto: University of Toronto Press, London: Routledge and Kegan Paul, 1963–91), 1.151.

31 Ibid., 1.157.

32 'The "Spirit of the Age" is in some measure a novel expression. I do not believe that it is to be met with in any work exceeding fifty years in antiquity. The idea of comparing one's own age with former ages, or with our notion of those which are yet to come, had occurred to philosophers; but it never before was itself the dominant idea of any age.' John Stuart Mill, 'The Spirit of the Age' (1831), *Collected Works*, 22.228.

33 Thomas Carlyle, *The French Revolution*, 3 vols. (1.2.7 *'Contrat Social'*), in *The Works of Thomas Carlyle*, ed. H. D. Traill, 30 vols. (London: Chapman and Hall, 1896–9), 2.55.

34 Thomas Carlyle, 'Thoughts on History', *Fraser's Magazine*, 2 (1830), 415; in *Thomas Carlyle: Historical Essays*, ed. Chris R. Vanden Bossche (Berkeley, Los Angeles and London: University of California Press, 2002), p. 7.

35 Thomas Carlyle, *Past and Present* (Bk. 2, ch. 8), eds. Chris R. Vanden Bossche, Joel J. Brattin and D. J. Trela (Berkeley, Los Angeles and London: University of California Press, 2005), p. 83.

36 Thomas Carlyle, *Past and Present* (Bk. 2, ch. 2), p. 53.

37 Robert Browning, *The Ring and the Book* (Bk. 1, 35–6); in *The Complete Works of Robert Browning*, eds. Jack W. Herring, Roma A. King, Park Honan, A. N. Kincaid, and Allan C. Dooley, 16 vols. (Athens, Ohio: Ohio University Press, 1969–98), 7.34–5.

38 J. A. Froude, 'History: Its Use and Meaning', rev. of Carlyle's *Past and Present*, 2nd edn, *Westminster Review*, 62 (1854), 423; quoted in Richard W. Schoch, '"We Do Nothing But Enact History": Thomas Carlyle Stages the Past', *Nineteenth-Century Literature* vol. 54, No. 1 (Jun. 1999), 27–52; 28.

39 *Ceterum censeo*: 'but I'm of the opinion'.

40 Friedrich Nietzsche, 'On the Uses and Disadvantages of History for Life' (1873), *Untimely Meditations*, ed. Daniel Breazedale, trans. R. J. Hollingdale (Cambridge: Cambridge University Press, 1997), p. 59.

41 Ibid., p. 82.

42 Ibid., p. 118.

43 Matthew Arnold, 'The Buried Life' (64–6); in *The Poems of Matthew Arnold*, ed. Kenneth Allott (London: Longmans, Green & Co., 1965), p. 274.

44 Arnold, 'Memorial Verses: April 1850' (44), *Poems*, p. 228.

45 Ibid., (4), p. 226.

46 Ibid., (62–7), p. 229.

47 Arnold, 'Empedocles on Etna' (Act 2, 327–30); *Poems*, p. 188.

48 Ibid. (Act 2, 394–6), p. 191.

49 Arnold, 'Preface to the First Edition of *Poems* (1853)', *Poems*, p. 591.

50 Arnold, 'Dover Beach' (37); *Poems*, p. 243.

51 See above, pp. 7–8.

52 Matthew Arnold, 'The Twice-Revised Code', *Fraser's Magazine* 65 (March 1862), 347–65; see *Prose Works*, 2.235.

53 Bruce Douglas, former President of the Secondary Heads' Association, October 1998; quoted in the Green Paper *Teachers: Meeting the Challenge of Change* (December 1998), Chapter 3, p. 33.

54 Arnold, 'Literature and Science', from *Discourses in America* (1885), *Prose Works*, 10.57.

55 Ibid., 10.57.

56 Ibid., 10.63.

57 Ibid., 10.65.

58 Arnold, 'Literature and Dogma' (1873), *Prose Works*, 6.176.

59 Arnold, *Prose Works*, 10.70.

60 Ibid., 10.71.

61 Ibid., 10.71.

62 Ibid., 10.64.

63 Sydney Smith, 'Professional Education' (1809), *The Works of Sydney Smith*, 3 vols. (London: Longman, Brown, Green and Longmans, 1854), 1.358. Smith was writing for the *Edinburgh Review*, a periodical which was consistently hostile to the Oxford classicism represented in Matthew Arnold's work.

64 Charles Dickens, *A Christmas Carol*, in *A Christmas Carol and other Christmas Books*, ed. Robert Douglas-Fairhurst (Oxford: Oxford University Press, 2006), p. 61.

65 Ibid, p. 62.

66 Charles Dickens, *The Speeches of Charles Dickens*, ed. K. J. Fielding (Oxford: Clarendon Press, 1960), p. 63. The phrase 'the one thing needful' is a Biblical quotation, also frequently cited by Matthew Arnold: '[Jesus] . . . entered into a certain village: and a certain woman named Martha received him into her house./And she had a sister called Mary . . . /But Martha was cumbered about much serving, and came to him, and said, Lord, dost thou not care that my sister hath left me to serve alone? Bid her therefore that she help me./And Jesus answered and said unto her, Martha, Martha, thou art careful and troubled about many things:/But one thing is needful: and Mary hath chosen that good part, which shall not be taken away from her.' Luke 10:38–42 (King James Bible).

67 Dickens, *A Christmas Carol*, p. 77.

68 Ibid., p. 9.

69 Ibid., p. 31.

70 Ibid.

71 Ibid.

72 Dickens, *The Old Curiosity Shop*, ed. Elizabeth M. Brennan (Oxford: Clarendon Press, 1997), p. 344.

73 Ibid., p. 345.

74 Dickens, *Dombey and Son*, ed. Alan Horsman (Oxford: Clarendon Press, 1974), p. 143.

75 Charles Dickens, *Our Mutual Friend*, ed. Michael Cotsell (Oxford, Oxford University Press, 1989), p. 219.

76 James Kay-Shuttleworth, *Minutes of Committee of Council on Education* (1842–3), p. 198.

77 Dickens, *Our Mutual Friend*, p. 340.

78 Ibid., p. 793.

79 Ibid., p. 800.

80 Dickens, *The Haunted Man*, in *A Christmas Carol and Other Christmas Books*, p. 326.

81 Ibid., pp. 325–6.

82 Ibid., p. 326.

83 Ibid., p. 399.

Chapter 2   Religious Learning

1 Frank M. Turner gives a cogent account of this revision in 'The Religious and the Secular in Victorian Britain', in *Contesting Cultural Authority: Essays in Victorian Cultural Life* (Cambridge: Cambridge University Press, 1993), pp. 3–38.

2 William Wilberforce to Hannah More, January 8, 1824, in Robert Wilberforce and Samuel Wilberforce, *The Life of William Wilberforce*, 5 vols. (London: John Murray, 1838), 5.211.

3 Elizabeth Missing Sewell, *Katharine Ashton*, 2 vols. (London: Longman, Brown, Green and Longmans, 1854), 1.333.

4 Ibid., 1.125.

5 George Herbert, 'The Church-porch' (56.331), *The Temple*, in *The Works of George Herbert*, ed. F. E. Hutchinson (Oxford: Clarendon Press, 1941), p. 19.

6 Charles Dickens, *Bleak House*, ed. Stephen Gill (Oxford: Oxford University Press, 1996), pp. 289–90.

7 Anthony Trollope, *Rachel Ray*, ed. P. D. Edwards (Oxford: Oxford University Press), pp. 77–8.

8   Trollope, *Barchester Towers*, eds. Michael Sadleir and Frederick Page (Oxford: Oxford University Press, 1996), p. 29.

9   Ibid., p. 30.

10 Sewell, *Katharine Ashton*, 1.206.

11 Sydney Smith, *The Works of Sydney Smith*, 3 vols. (London: Longman, Brown, Green and Longmans, 1854), 1.367.

12 A. R. Ashwell and R. G. Wilberforce, *The Life of Samuel Wilberforce* (London: Murray, 1883), p. 155; quoted in John T. Smith, ' "Merely a Growing Dilemma of Etiquette?": The Deepening Gulf between the Victorian Clergyman and Victorian Schoolteacher', *History of Education*, 33.2 March 2004, 155.

13 Letter to Edward Clayton, 18 August 1845, John Ruskin, *The Works of Ruskin*, eds. E. T. Cook and Alexander Wedderburn, (London: George Allen, 1903–12), 1.499.

14 Ibid., 35.185.

15 Ibid., 12.143.

16 Charlotte Brontë, *Shirley*, eds. Herbert Rosengarten and Margaret Smith, 1979 (Oxford: Clarendon Press, 1979), p. 7.

17 George Gissing, *Born in Exile*, ed. David Grylls (London: J. M. Dent, 1993), p. 24.

18 Thomas Hardy, *Jude the Obscure*, ed. Patricia Ingham (Oxford: Oxford University Press, 1998), p. 110.

19 Ibid., p. 32.

20 Arthur Stanley, *The Life and Correspondence of Thomas Arnold*, 2 vols. (London: B. Fellowes, 1845), 1.402.

21 Ibid., 1.95.

22 Thomas Arnold, *The Christian Life: Its Course, its Hindrances, and its Helps*, Sermon 1 (London: B. Fellowes, 1841), p. 7.

23 See below, pp. 79–89.

24 See above, pp. 19–23.

25 Thomas Hughes, *Tom Brown's Schooldays*, ed. Andrew Sanders (Oxford: Oxford University Press, 1989), pp. 73–4.

26 Ibid., p. 217.

27 Ibid., pp. 238–42.

28 Ibid., p. xxxix.

29 Ibid., p. 313.

30 John Henry Newman, 'Preface', *The Idea of a University*, ed. Frank M. Turner (New Haven and London: Yale University Press, 1996), p. 7.

31 Ibid., pp. 7–8.

32 Ibid., pp. 8–9.

33 Enthymeme: an argument based on merely probable grounds; a rhetorical argument as distinguished from a demonstrative one.

34 Newman, 'Preface', *The Idea of a University*, pp. 84–5.
35 Letter to Charles Bray, 25 November 1859: 'We are reading Darwin's Book of Species, just come out, after long expectation. It is an elaborate exposition of the evidence in favour of the Development Theory, and so, makes an epoch.' George Eliot, *The George Eliot Letters*, ed. Gordon S. Haight, 9 vols. (New Haven and London: Yale University Press, 1954–78), 3.214.
36 John Henry Newman, 'The Theory of Developments in Religious Doctrines' (Oxford University Sermons, 15, 2 February, 1843), *Sermons and Discourses (1839–57)*, ed. Charles Frederick Harrold (London: Longmans, Green & Co., 1949), p. 67.
37 Ibid., pp. 67–8.
38 John Henry Newman, *An Essay on the Development of Christian Doctrine*, rev. edn. (London: Basil Montagu Pickering, 1878), p. 36.
39 John Ruskin, *The Works of Ruskin*, eds. E. T. Cook and Alexander Wedderburn, (London: George Allen, 1903–12), 3.278–80.
40 Revelation, 21.21.
41 2 Chronicles 3.14.
42 Ruskin, *Works*, 9.xxviii.
43 Ibid., 11.65–6.
44 Ibid., 9.291; see below, pp. 140–2.

Chapter 3   Teaching Women

1 See above, pp. 33–6.
2 Kate Millett's *Sexual Politics* (New York: Doubleday, 1970) was foremost in early feminist attacks on Ruskin; for counter-arguments, see the essays assembled in *Ruskin and Gender*, eds. Dinah Birch and Francis O'Gorman (Houndmills: Palgrave, 2002).
3 John Ruskin, *The Works of Ruskin*, eds. E. T. Cook and Alexander Wedderburn, (London: George Allen, 1903–12), 18.126.
4 See Christina de Bellaigue, 'Teaching as a Profession for Women', *The Historical Journal*, 44, 4 (2001), 963–88; Mary Hilton, 'Revisioning Romanticism: Towards a Women's History of Progressive Thought 1780–1850', *History of Education*, 30, 5 (2001), 471–87; Mary Hilton and Pamela Hirsch, eds., *Practical Visionaries: Women, Education, and Social Progress, 1790–1930* (Harlow: Longman, 2000).
5 Useful works in this field would include Dina Copelman, *London's Women Teachers: Gender, Class and Feminism, 1870–1930* (London: Routledge and Kegan Paul, 1996); C. Dyhouse, *Girls Growing Up in Late Victorian and*

Edwardian England (London: Routledge and Kegan Paul, 1981); Jane Martin, *Women and the Politics of Schooling in Victorian and Edwardian England* (London and New York: Leicester University Press, 1999); Joyce Sanders Pedersen, *The Reform of Girls' Secondary Education in Victorian England: A Study of Elites and Educational Change* (London and New York: Garland, 1987).

6 Jane Austen, *Emma* (1816), eds. Richard Cronin and Dorothy McMillan (Cambridge: Cambridge University Press, 2005), p. 21.

7 Ibid.

8 Ibid.

9 George Eliot, *Middlemarch*, ed. David Carroll (Oxford: Clarendon Press, 1986), p. 94.

10 Significant contributions include W. R. Greg, 'Why are Women Redundant?', *National Review*, 14 (April 1862), 433–5, and Frances Power Cobbe, 'What Shall We Do With Our Old Maids?', *Fraser's Magazine*, 66 (November 1862), 594–610.

11 Sheridan Le Fanu, *Uncle Silas*, eds. W. J. McCormack and Andrew Swarbrick (Oxford: Oxford University Press, 1981), p. 18.

12 See Christina de Bellaigue, 966–8.

13 Ruskin's relations with Winnington Hall are described in Van Akin Burd, ed., *The Winnington Letters: John Ruskin's Correspondence with Margaret Alexis Bell and the Children of Winnington Hall* (Cambridge MA: Harvard University Press, 1969).

14 For a full account of the history of this school, see John Chapple, *Elizabeth Gaskell: The Early Years* (Manchester and New York: Manchester University Press, 1997), pp. 238–50.

15 George Eliot, *The Mill on The Floss* (1860), ed. Gordon S. Haight (Oxford: Clarendon Press, 1986), pp. 122–3.

16 'Letters to the Industrious Classes: Letter IV – To the Governesses of the United Kingdom' *Reynolds' Miscellany* (1846), 368; quoted in Christina de Bellaigue, 972.

17 Christina de Bellaigue, pp. 970–1.

18 Henry Morley, 'Infant Gardens', *Household Words* 11 (21 July 1855), 577–82.

19 See Mary Hilton, pp. 479–82.

20 Bertha Maria von Marenholtz-Buelow, *Women's Educational Mission: Being an Explanation of Friedrich Froebel's System of Infant Gardens*, trans. Countess Krockow von Wickerode (London: Dalton, 1855), p. 22.

21 Dorothea Beale, 'Girls' Schools Past and Present', *Nineteenth Century* 25 (April 1888), 545; quoted in Christina de Bellaigue, p. 978.

22 See Joyce Senders Pedersen, 'Schoolmistresses and Headmistresses: Elites and Education in Nineteenth-Century England', in *Women Who Taught: Perspectives on the History of Women and Teaching*, eds. Alison Prentice and Marjorie R. Theobald (Toronto and London: University of Toronto Press, 1991), p. 62n.

23 Governors' Report, Cheltenham Ladies' College, 1854.

24 Quoted in Janet Gough, 'Frances Buss', *Dictionary of National Biography* (Oxford: Oxford University Press, 1995).

25 Juliet Barker, *The Brontës* (London: Weidenfeld and Nicolson, 1994), p. 2.

26 Maria Branwell, letter to Patrick Brontë, 18 Sept 1812, quoted in Barker, *The Brontës*, p. 53.

27 See Barker, *The Brontës*, pp. 118–28.

28 Charlotte Brontë, *The Professor* (1845–6; pub. 1857), eds. Margaret Smith and Herbert Rosengarten (Oxford: Clarendon Press, 1987), p. 249.

29 Ibid. p. 247.

30 Brontë, 'Emma', repr. as appendix to *The Professor*, p. 303.

31 Ibid., p. 307.

32 Reproduced in Barker, *The Brontës*, facing p. 685; see pp. 439–41 for an account of the sisters' plan to open a school.

33 Charlotte Brontë, *Villette* (1853), eds. Margaret Smith and Herbert Rosengarten (Oxford: Clarendon Press, 1984), p. 702.

34 Ibid., p. 712.

35 Brontë, *Shirley*, eds. Herbert Rosengarten and Margaret Smith (Oxford: Clarendon Press, 1979), p. 712.

36 Brontë, *Villette*, pp. 700–1.

37 Ibid., p. 714.

38 Ellen Wood, *Mrs Halliburton's Troubles*, 3 vols. (London: Richard Bentley, 1862), 2.135.

39 Ibid., 2.141.

40 See Mary Poovey, 'The Anathematized Race: The Governess and *Jane Eyre*', in *Uneven Developments: The Ideological Work of Gender in Mid-Victorian England* (London: Virago, 1989), pp. 126–64, for a full account of this issue. A useful account of fictional responses is given in Cecilia Wadso Lecaros, *The Victorian Governess Novel* (Lund: Lund University Press, 2001); see also Kathryn Hughes, *The Victorian Governess* (London and Rio Grande: The Hambledon Press, 1993), and M. Jeanne Peterson, 'The Victorian Governess: Status Incongruence in Family and Society', in Martha Vicinus ed., *Suffer and Be Still: Women in the Victorian Age* (Bloomington: Indiana University Press, 1972), pp. 3–19.

41 Letter to Emily Brontë, 8 June 1839; quoted in Barker, *The Brontës*, p. 310.

42 Ellen Wood, *Mrs Halliburton's Troubles*, 3.344.

43 Elizabeth Sewell, *Principles of Education*, 2 vols. (London: Longman, 1865), 2.205.

44 Ibid., 1.30.

45 Ibid., 1.84.

46 Ibid., 2.228.

47 Ibid., 2.257.

48   Ibid., 2.261.

49   Ibid., 1.i.

50   Elizabeth Sewell, *Katharine Ashton*, 2 vols. (London: Longman, 1854), 2.308.

51   Elizabeth Sewell, *The Experience of Life*, 1853 (new edn., London: Longman, 1886), p. 15.

52   Elizabeth Sewell, *The Autobiography of Elizabeth Sewell*, ed. Eleanor L. Sewell (London: Longman, 1907), pp. 131–2.

53   Elizabeth Sewell, *After Life* (London: Longmans, Green & Co., 1868), p. 471.

54   Elizabeth Sewell, *The Journal of a Home Life*, 2 vols. (London: Longmans, Green & Co., 1867), 1.1.

55   George Eliot, letter to Harriet Beecher Stowe, 29 Oct. 1876, *Letters*, 6.302.

56   George Eliot, *Daniel Deronda*, ed. Graham Handley (Oxford: Clarendon Press, 1984), p. 161.

57   George Eliot, *Adam Bede*, ed. Carol. A. Martin (Oxford: Clarendon Press, 2001), p. 159.

58   George Eliot, *The Lifted Veil, and Brother Jacob*, ed. Helen Small (Oxford: Oxford University Press, 1999), p. 6.

59   George Eliot, *Middlemarch*, p. 239.

60   Ibid., p. 238.

61   George Eliot, 'Margaret Fuller and Mary Wollstonecraft', George Eliot, *Leader*, vi (13 Oct. 1855), 988–9; in *George Eliot: Selected Writings*, ed. Rosemary Ashton (Oxford: Oxford University Press, 1992), p. 183.

62   George Eliot, *The Mill on the Floss*, p. 17.

63   George Eliot, 'Margaret Fuller and Mary Wollstonecraft', p. 185.

64   George Eliot, *Daniel Deronda*, pp. 34–5.

65   George Eliot, *Middlemarch*, p. 8.

66   Ibid., p. 24.

67   Ibid., p. 17.

68   Ibid., p. 73.

69   Ibid., p. 190.

70   Ibid., p. 818.

71   Ibid.

72   Ibid., p. 819.

73   George Eliot, *The Mill on the Floss*, p. 252.

74   George Eliot, 'Thomas Carlyle', *Leader*, vi (27 Oct. 1855), 1034–5; in *Selected Writings*, p. 187.

75   George Eliot, *Daniel Deronda*, p. 338.

76   George Eliot, letter to Sara Hennell, 27 Nov. 1847, *Letters*, 1.242.

77   George Eliot, letter to Maria Lewis, 20 May 1841, *Letters*, 1.91.

78   George Eliot, letter to Mrs Nassau John Senior, 4 Oct. 1869, *Letters*, 5.57.

79   George Eliot, letter to Emily Davis, 8 Aug. 1868, *Letters*, 4.468.

80 George Eliot, *The Mill on the Floss*, p. 417.
81 George Eliot, *Daniel Deronda*, p. 336.
82 Ruskin, *Works*, 18.131.
83 Elizabeth Barrett Browning, *Aurora Leigh* (Bk. 1, 815–17), ed. Kerry McSweeny (Oxford: Oxford University Press, 1993), p. 28.

Chapter 4 New Conversations

1 Tony Blair, speech delivered at Ruskin College, Oxford, 16 December 1996. Ruskin College is an independent college which specializes in providing educational opportunities for adults with few or no qualifications.
2 David Miliband, from a speech in Newcastle by the schools minister to an Institute for Public Policy Research conference on social mobility (*Independent*, 8 September 2003).
3 Matthew Arnold, 'Preface', *Culture and Anarchy* (1869, *The Complete Prose Works of Matthew Arnold*, ed. R. H. Super, 11 vols. (Ann Arbor: University of Michigan Press, 1960–77), 5.530–1.
4 Ibid., 5.531.
5 Alan Johnson MP, debate on Budget Resolutions and Economic Situation, *Hansard (Commons)*, 22 March 2007, column 977.
6 Matthew Arnold, *Literature and Dogma* (1873), *Prose Works*, 6.189.
7 See above, pp. 12–19.
8 John Keats, letter to George and Georgiana Keats, 14 Feb.–4 May 1819, *Selected Letters of John Keats*, ed. Grant F. Scott (Cambridge, MA and London: Harvard University Press, 2002), p. 291.
9 Matthew Arnold, *Prose Works*, 10.176.
10 See above, p. 104.
11 Elizabeth Missing Sewell, *The Journal of a Home Life* (London: Longmans, Green & Co., 1867), 1.66.
12 See above, pp. 21–3.
13 Thomas Carlyle, 'Signs of the Times', in *Critical and Miscellaneous Essays* (II), *The Works of Thomas Carlyle*, ed. H. D. Traill, 30 vols. (London: Chapman and Hall, 1896–9), 27.59.
14 Ibid., 27.61. The 'Lancastrian' scheme, devised by Joseph Lancaster (1778–1838) used the monitorial system, in which older pupils taught younger ones, meaning that a small body of adult teachers could manage the teaching of large numbers of children. James Hamilton, 1769–1829, was the inventor of the 'Hamiltonian' system, a method of teaching languages based on interlineal, literal translation of a text rather than the use of grammar and dictionary.

15 Etymology: the study of the derivation of words.
16 Thomas Carlyle, *Sartor Resartus*, eds. Rodger Tarr and Mark Engel (Berkeley, Los Angeles and London: University of California Press, 2000), pp. 81–2.
17 Ibid., p. 137.
18 Thomas Carlyle, 'Inaugural Address at Edinburgh' (1866), in *Critical and Miscellaneous Essays* (IV), *Works*, 29.466.
19 Ibid., 29.475.
20 Ibid., 29.466.
21 See above, pp. 68–75.
22 John Ruskin, *The Works of Ruskin*, eds. E. T. Cook and Alexander Wedderburn, (London: George Allen, 1903–12), 18.23.
23 Ibid., 7.207.
24 Ruskin's serial letters to the 'workmen and labourers of Great Britain' (1871–84).
25 John Ruskin, *Works*, 27.152.
26 Thomas Carlyle, 'Inaugural Address', *Works*, 29.474.
27 William Wordsworth, *The Excursion* (IV.764), in *Wordsworth's Poetical Works*, eds. Ernest de Selincourt and Helen Darbishire, 5 vols. (Oxford: Oxford University Press, 1940–9), 5.133.
28 John Ruskin, *Works*, 28.255.
29 Ibid., 16.154.
30 John Ruskin, 'Modern Education', in *The Stones of Venice* III, *Works*, 11.261.
31 Ibid., 11.258–9.
32 Ibid., 11.262. Cf. Nietzsche: 'Forgetting is essential to action of any kind, just as not only light but darkness too is essential for the life of everything organic' ('On the Uses and Disadvantages of History for Life', *Untimely Meditations*, p. 62).
33 See above, pp. 71–3.
34 See above, pp. 70–1.
35 Keats, letter to George and Tom Keats, 21–27 Dec. 1817, *Selected Letters*, p. 60.
36 George Eliot, letter to Barbara Bodichon, 5 December 1859, *Letters*, 3.227.
37 George Eliot, *The Lifted Veil, and Brother Jacob*, ed. Helen Small (Oxford: Oxford University Press, 1999), p. 29.
38 Morris reprinted the chapter among the first productions of his pioneering Kelmscott Press, founded to demonstrate the artistic potential of the highest standards of printing and binding in book production.
39 John Ruskin, *Works*, 10.190.
40 Ibid., 10.190–3.
41 Ibid., 10.194.

Bibliography

Anderson, Robert (2006) *British Universities: Past and Present*. London: Hambledon Continuum.

Anonymous (1846) 'Letters to the Industrious Classes: Letter IV – To the Governesses of the United Kingdom', *Reynolds' Miscellany*, 368.

Arnold, Matthew (1960–77) *The Complete Prose Works of Matthew Arnold*, 11 vols., ed. R. H. Super. Ann Arbor: University of Michigan Press.

Arnold, Matthew (1965) *The Poems of Matthew Arnold*, ed. Kenneth Allott. London: Longmans, Green & Co.

Arnold, Thomas (1841) *The Christian Life: Its Course, its Hindrances, and its Helps*. London: B. Fellowes.

Austen, Jane (2005) *Emma*, eds. Richard Cronin and Dorothy McMillan. Cambridge: Cambridge University Press.

Bamford, T. W. (1967) *The Rise of the Public Schools*. London: Nelson.

Barker, Juliet (1994) *The Brontës*. London: Weidenfeld and Nicolson.

Barrett Browning, Elizabeth (1993) *Aurora Leigh*, ed. Kerry McSweeny. Oxford: Oxford University Press.

Beale, Dorothea (1888) 'Girls' Schools Past and Present', *Nineteenth Century* 25, 541–54.

de Bellaigue, Christina (2001) 'Teaching as a Profession for Women', *The Historical Journal* 44: 963–88.

Birch, Dinah and O'Gorman, Francis (eds.) (2002) *Ruskin and Gender*. Houndmills: Palgrave.

Brontë, Charlotte (1979) *Shirley*, eds. Herbert Rosengarten and Margaret Smith. Oxford: Clarendon Press.

Brontë, Charlotte (1984) *Villette*, eds. Herbert Rosengarten and Margaret Smith. Oxford: Clarendon Press.

Brontë, Charlotte (1987) *The Professor*, eds. Herbert Rosengarten and Margaret Smith. Oxford: Clarendon Press.

Bibliography

Browning, Robert (1969–98) *The Ring and the Book*, in Jack W. Herring, Roma A. King, Park Honan, A. N. Kincaid and Allan C. Dooley (eds.), *The Complete Works of Robert Browning*, 16 vols. Athens, Ohio: Ohio University Press.

Burd, Van Akin (ed.) (1969) *The Winnington Letters: John Ruskin's Correspondence with Margaret Alexis Bell and the Children of Winnington Hall*. Cambridge, MA: Harvard University Press.

Carlyle, Thomas (1896–9) *The French Revolution*, 3 vols., in H. D. Traill (ed.), *The Works of Thomas Carlyle*, 30 vols. London: Chapman and Hall.

Carlyle, Thomas (2000) *Sartor Resartus*, eds. Rodger Tarr and Mark Engel. Berkeley, Los Angeles and London: University of California Press.

Carlyle, Thomas (2002) 'Thoughts on History', *Fraser's Magazine*, 2 (1830); in Chris R Vanden Bossche (ed.) *Thomas Carlyle: Historical Essays*. Berkeley, Los Angeles and London: University of California Press.

Carlyle, Thomas (2005) *Past and Present*, eds. Chris R. Vanden Bossche, Joel J. Brattin, and D. J. Trela. Berkeley, Los Angeles and London: University of California Press.

Chapple, John (1997) *Elizabeth Gaskell: The Early Years*. Manchester and New York: Manchester University Press.

Cobbe, Frances Power (1862) 'What Shall We Do With Our Old Maids?', *Fraser's Magazine* 66: 594–610.

Copelman, Dina (1996) *London's Women Teachers: Gender, Class and Feminism, 1870–1930*. London: Routledge and Kegan Paul.

Department for Education and Employment (1998) *Teachers: Meeting the Challenge of Change*, cm 4164. London: Stationery Office.

Dickens, Charles (1960) *The Speeches of Charles Dickens*, ed. K. J. Fielding. Oxford: Clarendon Press.

Dickens, Charles (1974) *Dombey and Son*, ed. Alan Horsman. Oxford: Clarendon Press.

Dickens, Charles (1989) *Our Mutual Friend*, ed. Michael Cotsell. Oxford: Oxford University Press.

Dickens, Charles (1990) *Nicholas Nickleby*, ed. Paul Schlicke. Oxford: Oxford University Press.

Dickens, Charles (1996) *Bleak House*, ed. Stephen Gill. Oxford: Oxford University Press.

Dickens, Charles (1997) *The Old Curiosity Shop*, ed. Elizabeth M. Brennan. Oxford: Clarendon Press.

Dickens, Charles (2006) *A Christmas Carol*, in Robert Douglas-Fairhurst (ed.) *A Christmas Carol and Other Christmas Books*. Oxford: Oxford University Press.

Dyhouse, C. (1981) *Girls Growing Up in Late Victorian and Edwardian England*. London: Routledge and Kegan Paul.

Eliot, George (1954–78) *The George Eliot Letters*, 9 vols., ed. Gordon S. Haight. New Haven and London: Yale University Press.

Bibliography

Eliot, George (1984) *Daniel Deronda*, ed. Graham Handley. Oxford: Clarendon Press.

Eliot, George (1986) *Middlemarch*, ed. David Carroll. Oxford: Clarendon Press.

Eliot, George (1986) *The Mill on The Floss*, ed. Gordon S. Haight. Oxford: Clarendon Press.

Eliot, George (1992) 'Margaret Fuller and Mary Wollstonecraft', George Eliot, *Leader*, vi (13 Oct. 1855), 988–9; in Rosemary Ashton (ed.) *George Eliot: Selected Writings*. Oxford: Oxford University Press.

Eliot, George (1992) 'Thomas Carlyle', *Leader* vi (27 Oct. 1855), 1034–5; in Rosemary Ashton (ed.) *George Eliot: Selected Writings*. Oxford: Oxford University Press.

Eliot, George (1999) *The Lifted Veil, and Brother Jacob*, ed. Helen Small. Oxford: Oxford University Press.

Eliot, George (2001) *Adam Bede*, ed. Carol A. Martin. Oxford: Clarendon Press.

Froude, J. A (1854) 'History: Its Use and Meaning', rev. of Thomas Carlyle's *Past and Present*, 2nd edn., *Westminster Review* 62: 420–48.

Gill, Stephen (1998) *Wordsworth and the Victorians*. Oxford: Clarendon Press.

Gissing, George (1993) *Born in Exile*, ed. David Grylls. London: J. M. Dent.

Gough, Janet (1995) 'Frances Buss', *Dictionary of National Biography*. Oxford: Oxford University Press.

Greg, W. R. (1862) 'Why are Women Redundant?', *National Review* 14: 433–5.

Hardy, Thomas (1998) *Jude the Obscure*, ed. Patricia Ingham. Oxford: Oxford University Press.

Harrison, J. F. C. (1961) *Learning and Living*. London: Routledge and Kegan Paul.

Herbert, George (1941) *The Works of George Herbert*, ed. F. E. Hutchinson. Oxford: Clarendon Press.

Hilton, Mary (2001) 'Revisioning Romanticism: Towards a Women's History of Progressive Thought 1780–1850', *History of Education* 30, 471–87.

Hilton, Mary and Hirsch, Pamela (eds.) (2000) *Practical Visionaries: Women, Education, and Social Progress, 1790–1930*. Harlow: Longman.

Hughes, Kathryn (1993) *The Victorian Governess*. London and Rio Grande: The Hambledon Press.

Hughes, Thomas (1989) *Tom Brown's Schooldays*, ed. Andrew Sanders. Oxford: Oxford University Press.

Hurt, John (1971) *Education in Evolution*. London: Hart-Davis.

Johnson, Alan (2007) 'Debate on Budget Resolutions and Economic Situation', *Hansard (Commons)*, Thursday 22 March, column 977.

Keats, John (2002) *Selected Letters of John Keats*, ed. Grant F. Scott. Cambridge, MA and London: Harvard University Press.

Le Fanu, Sheridan (1981) *Uncle Silas*, eds. W. J. McCormack and Andrew Swarbrick. Oxford: Oxford University Press.

Bibliography

Lowe, Robert (1862) *Hansard (Commons)*, vol. 165, column 242.

Martin, Jane (1999) *Women and the Politics of Schooling in Victorian and Edwardian England*. London and New York: Leicester University Press.

Miliband, David (2003) Speech delivered at an Institute for Public Policy Research conference on social mobility in Newcastle. *The Independent*, 8 September.

Mill, John Stuart (1963–91) *Autobiography*, in J. M. Robson (ed.) *The Collected Works of John Stuart Mill*, 33 vols. Toronto: University of Toronto Press; London: Routledge and Kegan Paul.

Millett, Kate (1970) *Sexual Politics*. New York: Doubleday.

Morley, Henry (1855) 'Infant Gardens', *Household Words* 11, 21 July, 577–82.

Newman, John Henry (1878) *An Essay on the Development of Christian Doctrine*. Rev. edn., London: Basil Montagu Pickering.

Newman, John Henry (1949) 'The Theory of Developments in Religious Doctrines' (Oxford University Sermons, 15, 2nd February, 1843), in Charles Frederick Harrold (ed.) *Sermons and Discourses (1839–57)*. London: Longmans, Green & Co.

Newman, John Henry (1979) *A Grammar of Assent*, ed. Nicholas Lash. Notre Dame: University of Notre Dame Press.

Newman, John Henry (1996) *The Idea of a University*, ed. Frank M. Turner. New Haven and London: Yale University Press.

Nietzsche, Friedrich (1997) 'On the Uses and Disadvantages of History for Life', in Daniel Breazedale (ed.) and R. J. Hollingdale (trans.) *Untimely Meditations*. Cambridge: Cambridge University Press.

O'Gorman, Francis (ed.) (2004) *Victorian Poetry: An Annotated Anthology*. Oxford: Blackwell.

Peacock, Thomas Love (1987) *Headlong Hall and Gryll Grange*, eds. Michael Baron, and Michael Slater. Oxford: Oxford University Press.

Pedersen, Joyce Senders (1987) *The Reform of Girls' Secondary Education in Victorian England: A Study of Elites and Educational Change*. London and New York: Garland.

Pedersen, Joyce Senders (1991) 'Schoolmistresses and Headmistresses: Elites and Education in Nineteenth-Century England', in Alison Prentice and Marjorie Theobald (eds.), *Women Who Taught: Perspectives on the History of Women and Teaching*. Toronto and London: University of Toronto Press.

Peterson, M. Jeanne (1972) 'The Victorian Governess: Status Incongruence in Family and Society', in Vicinus Martha (ed.), *Suffer and Be Still: Women in the Victorian Age*. Bloomington: Indiana University Press.

Poovey, Mary (1989) *Uneven Developments: The Ideological Work of Gender in Mid-Victorian England*. London: Virago.

Roach, John (1986) *A History of Secondary Education in England, 1800–1870*. London: Longman.

Bibliography

Rothblatt, Sheldon (1968) *The Revolution of the Dons: Cambridge and Society in Victorian England.* London: Faber.

Ruskin, John (1903–12) *The Works of Ruskin*, 39 vols., eds. E. T. Cook and Alexander Wedderburn. London: George Allen.

Schoch, Richard (1999) ' "We Do Nothing But Enact History": Thomas Carlyle Stages the Past', *Nineteenth-Century Literature* 54: 27–52.

Scott, Patrick and Pauline Fletcher (1990) *Culture and Education in Victorian England.* London: Bucknell University Press.

Sewell, Elizabeth Missing (1854) *Katharine Ashton*, 2 vols. London: Longman, Brown, Green and Longmans.

Sewell, Elizabeth Missing (1865) *Principles of Education*, 2 vols. London: Longman.

Sewell, Elizabeth Missing (1867) *The Journal of a Home Life*, 2 vols. London: Longmans, Green & Co.

Sewell, Elizabeth Missing (1868) *After Life.* London: Longmans, Green & Co.

Sewell, Elizabeth Missing (1886) *The Experience of Life.* New edn., London: Longman.

Sewell, Elizabeth Missing (1907) *The Autobiography of Elizabeth Sewell*, ed. Eleanor L. Sewell. London: Longman.

Smith, John (2004) ' "Merely a Growing Dilemma of Etiquette?": The Deepening Gulf between the Victorian Clergyman and Victorian Schoolteacher', *History of Education* 33: 157–76.

Smith, Sydney (1854) *The Works of Sydney Smith*, 3 vols. London: Longman, Brown, Green and Longmans.

Smithser, Neil (1991) *Social Paralysis and Social Change: British Working-Class Education in the Nineteenth Century.* Berkeley: University of California Press.

Stanley, Arthur (1845) *The Life and Correspondence of Thomas Arnold*, 2 vols. London: B. Fellowes.

Stephens, W. B. (1998) *Education in Britain, 1750–1914.* New York: St Martins Press.

Sutherland, Gillian (1971) *Elementary Education in the Nineteenth Century.* London: Historical Association.

Tennyson, Alfred (1987) *The Poems of Tennyson*, 3 vols., ed. Christopher Ricks. Harlow: Longman.

Trollope, Anthony (1980) *An Autobiography*, eds. Michael Sadleir and Frederick Page, with introduction and notes by P. D. Edwards. Oxford: Oxford University Press.

Trollope, Anthony (1996) *Barchester Towers*, eds. Michael Sadleir and Frederick Page. Oxford: Oxford University Press.

Trollope, Anthony (1998) *Rachel Ray*, ed. P. D. Edwards. Oxford: Oxford University Press.

Turner, Frank (1993) *Contesting Cultural Authority: Essays in Victorian Cultural Life.* Cambridge: Cambridge University Press.

Vincent, David (1989) *Literacy and Popular Culture.* Cambridge: Cambridge University Press.

von Marenholtz-Buelow, Bertha Maria (1855) *Women's Educational Mission: Being an Explanation of Friedrich Froebel's System of Infant Gardens*, trans. Countess Krockow von Wickerode. London: Dalton.

Wadso Lecaros, Cecilia (2001) *The Victorian Governess Novel*. Lund: Lund University Press.

Wardle, David (1976) *English Popular Education 1780–1975*. Cambridge: Cambridge University Press.

Wilberforce, Robert and Wilberforce, Samuel (1838) *The Life of William Wilberforce*, 5 vols., London: John Murray.

Wood, Ellen (1862) *Mrs Halliburton's Troubles*, 3 vols. London: Richard Bentley.

Wordsworth, William (1935) *The Early Letters of William Wordsworth*, ed. Ernest de Selincourt. Oxford: Oxford University Press.

Wordsworth, William (1940–9) *Wordsworth's Poetical Works*, 5 vols., eds. Ernest de Selincourt and Helen Darbishire. Oxford: Oxford University Press.

Wordsworth, William (1963) *Lyrical Ballads*, eds. R. L. Brett, and A. R. Jones. London: Methuen.

Wordsworth, William (1974) *The Prose Works of William Wordsworth*, 3 vols., eds. W. J. B. Owen and Jane Worthington Smyser. Oxford: Clarendon Press.

Index

164